About the Author

Born in Germany, Edgar Rothermich studied music and sound engineering at the prestigious Tonmeister program at the University of Arts in Berlin where he graduated in 1989 with a Master's Degree. He worked as a composer and music producer in Berlin and moved to Los Angeles in 1991 where he continued his work on numerous projects in the music and film industry ("The Celestine Prophecy", "Outer Limits", "Babylon 5", "What the Bleep do we know", "Fuel", "Big Money Rustlas").

For the past 20 years Edgar has had a successful musical partnership with electronic music pioneer and founding Tangerine Dream member Christopher Franke. Recently in addition to his collaboration with Christopher, Edgar has been working with other artists as well as on his own projects.

In 2010 he started to release his solo records in the "Why Not ..." series with different styles and genres. The current releases are "Why Not Solo Piano", "Why Not Electronica", "Why Not Electronica Again", and "Why Not 90s Electronica". This previously unreleased album was produced in 1991/1992 by Christopher Franke. All albums are available on Amazon and iTunes including the 2012 release, the re-recording of the Blade Runner Soundtrack.

In addition to composing music, Edgar Rothermich is writing technical manuals with a unique style, focusing on rich graphics and diagrams to explain concepts and functionality of software applications under his popular GEM series (Graphically Enhanced Manuals). His bestselling titles are available as printed books on Amazon, as Multi-Touch eBooks on the iBookstore and as pdf downloads from his website. (languages: English, Deutsch, Español, 简体中文)

www.DingDingMusic.com   GEM@DingDingMusic.com

About the GEM (Graphically Enhanced Manuals)

UNDERSTAND, not just LEARN

What are Graphically Enhanced Manuals? They're a new type of manual with a visual approach that helps you UNDERSTAND a program, not just LEARN it. No need to read through 500 of pages of dry text explanations. Rich graphics and diagrams help you to get that "aha" effect and make it easy to comprehend difficult concepts. The Graphically Enhanced Manuals help you master a program much faster with a much deeper understanding of concepts, features and workflows in a very intuitive way that is easy to understand.

About the Formatting

Green colored text indicates keyboard shortcuts. I use the following abbreviations: **sh** (shift key), **ctr** (control key), **opt** (option key), **cmd** (command key). A plus (+) between the keys means that you have to press all those keys at the same time. sh+opt+K means: hold the shift and the option and the K key at the same time.

Brown colored text indicates Menu Commands with a greater sign (➤) indicating submenus.
Edit ➤ Source Media ➤ All means Click on the Edit Menu, scroll down to Source Media and select "All" from the submenu.

Blue arrows indicate what happens if you click on an item or popup menu ●———➤

About the Editor

Many thanks to Chas Ferry for editing and proofreading my manuals. www.hollywoodtrax.com

The manual is based on Motion v5.0.7
Manual: Print Version 2013-0808

ISBN-13: 978-1475008784
ISBN-10: 1475008783

Table of Contents

1 - Introduction

The Approach

The difficult in writing a manual is in explaining an application's concept. This might require the use of existing and new terminology, plus other new concepts that first require an explanation. This leads one to pose the chicken-and-egg question, what comes first.

I personally find that many manuals make the simple mistake of explaining the topics in the wrong order. Starting right from the top, they show where to click in order get some fast results without developing an understanding of why to click there in the first place. It caters to the notion of instant gratification, be ready "in minutes" and work like a pro with a little "knowledge"..

Many content-creation applications are very "deep" and cannot be learned (and certainly not mastered) in minutes. Sometimes they require a previous understanding of the specific field (graphics, video, audio, design, etc). To avoid any struggle with an app which leads to frustration (a killer of any form of creativity), I look at a threefold learning process, a pyramid:

☑ **Foundation**
This is the level that everything is building on. You have to learn and understand the basics of the specific field and how it is applied to the specific software application. That involves the user interface with its commands and tools.

☑ **Content**
Many software packages come with a ton of content. That content in form of effects, specialized objects etc requires additional time to learn and to get familiar with.

☑ **Practice**
The last step is then just practice and experience, applying all that knowledge and understanding, learning tricks and workflows to become a true master.

In my Graphically Enhanced Manuals, I'm concentrating on the first level, trying to build the solid foundation that everything else depends on. This requires a proper understanding of the software application, how it functions and how to use it. Learning all the additional content can then be as easy as looking it up in the official documentation. No need to "re-print" that again. After that, you search for practice, tips and tricks, material which is widely available. Exchanging workflows and sharing your experience in forums and other forms leads to the last step of the life long learning process.

Back to the main problem. Especially in Motion, it is difficult to teach the content in a linear fashion, explaining the features one at a time and building the understanding of the program that way. This could lead to confusion because explaining a new topic is tricky if it requires the understanding of a related topic that hasn't been explained yet or is unfamiliar.

That's why I'm trying a different approach. I will often introduce basic concepts and the underlying mechanism of Motion first without showing any interface elements and specific tools of the app. This way, I can explain the terminology and concepts first and provide the necessary awareness and understanding what a motion-graphics application like Motion is. Then, when I show the specifics in Motion (its interface, tools and elements), we will not just learn "what" Motion is doing, but "how" it is doing and even "why" it is doing it. The explanations in any part of the manual will then be based on the developed understanding of that basic concept of a motion-graphics app. So let's get to it.

What is Motion

- The very first question is: What is Motion? -
    - the answer is: Motion is a motion-graphics application.
- The second question is: What is a motion-graphics application?
    - the answer is: A graphics application with an added *time* element.
- The third question is: What does that mean?
    - read on ...

Here is a simple diagram that compares a Graphics application to a Motion-Graphics application.

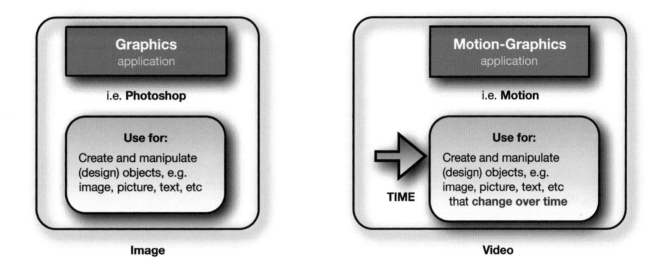

If you take Photoshop as the representation of a graphics application and compare it to Motion as the representation of a motion-graphics application, then you can see that both applications are doing practically the same thing. They let you design graphics, which means, using individual objects (the building blocks) and manipulating them in any form and shape to develop the final work. Those objects can be anything from pictures, images and often just shapes and text. The important thing is that in Photoshop these objects are "still images". They are not moving, no motion involved.

The Motion application however focuses not only on the manipulation of the individual objects, but the manipulation of those objects over time. This is where the "motion" part comes in. While in Photoshop, you try to create the best graphics (i.e. for a print media), in Motion you try to create the best *moving* graphics, a video.

Practical Use

You can use Photoshop or any other graphics application for a wide variety of tasks. For example, you can import a photo for editing, from minor correction up to extreme manipulation. But you can also create graphical elements from scratch like text or shapes in order to create new graphics. Or, combine both elements, photos and new graphics.

The same applies to Motion. There is not just one task that you can do with Motion. The area of motion-graphics covers a wide range, but what they all have in common is that "stuff is moving":

- Text based title sequences
- Visual Effects
- Animation
- Create all that in 2D or 3D

Apple's official documentation for Motion has over 1,400 pages which indicates how deep the program is. But regardless of what you use Motion for, the workflow and the tools are always the same. Once you understand those underlying concepts and get familiar with the basic tool set, then the rest is just practice and experience. The limit will be your own imagination.

What is Motion for

This is the next fundamental question after you know what Motion is and what it can do:
What is Motion for, what is its purpose?

There are two main purposes:

💡 Create a standalone Video file, based on motion-graphics effects

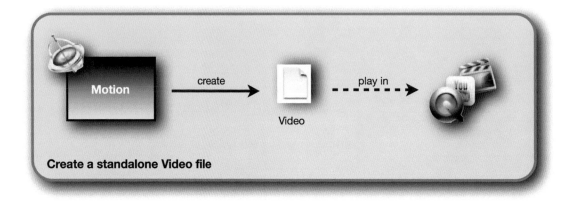

You can create a standalone video that is based on motion-graphics instead of just standard video footage. The end result, the finished video file, can end up as a standalone movie that you play in Quicktime, upload to YouTube or use as a video clip in FCPx as a segment of a bigger video production.

💡 Create a Template for FCPx that uses it as a motion-graphics effect

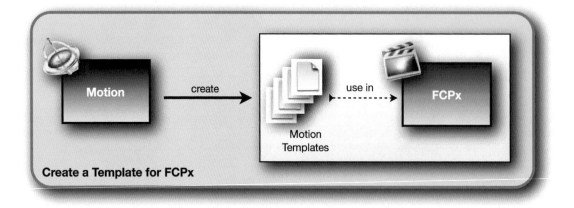

This is the second purpose of Motion. Motion functions as the delivery format for virtually all the graphics effects that are used in FCPx (Effects, Transitions, Titles, Generators). All those effects, that are available from the Media Browser in FCPx, are created in Motion and saved as Motion Templates. You can tweak those effects in Motion or create your own Motion Templates that you can use later in your FCPx projects. Many third party companies sell those Motion Templates for FCPx to end users so they can extend their Effects library in FCPx .

What is Motion's Material

Once you are ready to start creating your own Motion Project you might ask yourself, "with what elements can I create those motion-graphics?"

Here is a very simple diagram with the two main elements: **Objects** and **Tools**

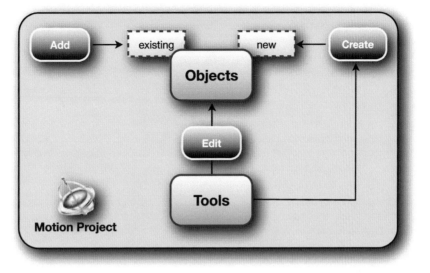

💡 **Objects**

   Virtually everything in your Project is an Object, an element that you **work on**

💡 **Tools**

   The tools are the elements that you **work with**. They let you create new Objects or manipulate existing ones.

Origin of Objects

The Objects in your Project originate from three different "sources".

💡 **From the Finder - *import***
   These are mainly media files that you import from your drive into your Project (video, images, audio)

💡 **From Motion - *apply***
   The Motion application ships with a huge collection of all kinds of ready to use Objects, everything from media files and computer-generated files up to a wide variety of effect Objects. Although they exist somewhere on your drive, they can only be accessed from inside the Motion app and applied to your Project.

💡 **From Scratch - *create***
   These are new Objects that you create from scratch in your current Project with the tools that the Motion app provides. Those Objects include a wide variety of shapes and text.

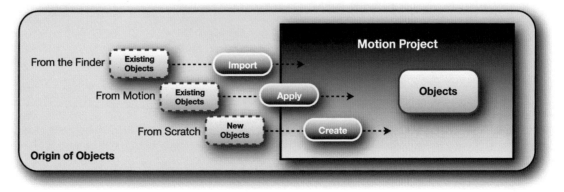

Terminology

As with any other application, there is a special "language", the use of specific terminology to describe tools and procedures. Some terms are app specific but many terms are common in the field the app is for. For example, ProTools (sound recording), Logic (music composition), Photoshop (graphics, illustration), FCPx (video editing). Learning any of those apps first requires a basic understanding of that subject (and its related terminology) before using the app itself.

That means, we will encounter two kinds of terminology:

☑ **Motion-graphics terminology**

> Those technical terms might or might not be familiar to the reader based on his or her previous knowledge.

☑ **Motion terminology**

> Those app specific terms are not a problem because that is what this manual is for.

A potential Motion user (and reader of this manual) can be someone who used previous versions or has experience with other motion-graphics applications. Those users might know the basics like "Alpha Channel", "Bezier Curves" or "Keyframes" very well and they just want to learn how Motion is incorporating those tools or what other new tools and techniques Motion is providing.

On the other end of the user spectrum, there could be the novice user with very little background of motion-graphics who wants to use the application to start in that field. That user might have a different set of initial questions, like "what is an "Alpha Channel?", "What are Bezier Curves or Keyframes"?

Usually, a manual will provide a Glossary at the end with short descriptions of important terminology to provide the necessary foundation for the topic. I will try a different approach. In this chapter, I list the most important terms with the short description first. This way, I can point out the areas that need a basic understanding in order to learn the application (an additional Google search or Wikipedia lookup is recommended if that subject is somewhat new to you).

As I mentioned earlier, it is difficult to teach a "deep" program like Motion in a linear way. By introducing the key elements upfront, I can use those terms if necessary in the context of a different topic even if I explain that term and its function in its own section in more detail later in the book.

Motion-Graphics Terms

💡 Composition - Compositing

Composition is just another word for the actual Project you are working on. The word means "putting stuff together". In that context, put your elements (the building blocks of your project) together, arrange them, tweak and manipulate them until your motion-graphics looks the way you want it.

Compositing is the process of putting two (or more) images together. The main focus is on "how do they interact?". This can be as simple as placing two images next to each other. If you place them on top of each other (i.e. text on picture), then you have to decide if they block each other or if there will be transparency. More complex compositing involves merging live actors together with animated images and background images with green screens or multiple layers in an animation sequence.

In Motion, you build a Composition in your Motion Project. Although there is a slight difference in Motion between a Project and a Composition, I use both terms in the same context as your "Motion creation".

💡 Opacity - Transparency - Blend

Each physical object has specific properties that determine what happens when you shine a light on it. It will block it (opaque), it will let some light through (translucent) or it will let all light through (transparent). The same principle is applied when putting image A on top of image B. Image B represents the light and image A is the Object in question. Will it block image B (100% Opacity) or will it let image B shine through (100% Transparency). Usually an application provides a slider for either opacity or transparency because they express the inverse value (100% transparency is 0% opacity and vice versa).

When you place two images on top of each other with some level of transparency, you are actually "blending" those two images together. Most graphics applications provide many different "Blend Modes" that set specific rules for the transparency. Those blend modes combined with the amount of transparency offer a wide range of image manipulation.

Alpha Channel - Masking

"Create an alpha channel" or *"an image has an alpha channel"* means that a specific color in that picture or specific pixels in that picture have been marked to be treated with full transparency. Putting an image A with an alpha channel on top of image B, will let image B "shine through" the areas that are marked with an alpha channel. The other areas are non transparent. The result is that the non-marked areas of image A are "floating" on top of image B.

A Mask is used in a similar way. This time however, you create a shape (circle, rectangle, freeform or even text). This will be our image A that sits on top the image we apply the mask to (image B). The result is that everything inside that shape will be transparent and everything outside the shape will be blocked. An inverse button can flip that behavior.

Bitmap graphics - Vector-based graphics - Rasterization

A typical image file (jpeg, tiff) is a bitmap graphic, i.e. a picture of a circle. Like on an old-fashioned newspaper, if you zoom in very closely, you see that the image is made up of thousands or millions of little dots of different colors. It looks like a raster or a matrix. The amount of the available bits (pixels) represents the resolution of the image. Any manipulation of such an image in a graphics application is restricted to the manipulation of those bits. For example, you can change the colors (filter) or the arrangement (transform, distort) of those bits.

A vector-based graphic on the other hand is a set of mathematical instructions that tells the computer what to "draw". That's why they are also called *computer graphics* or *computer generated*. The big advantage is that when you manipulate that graphic, you are not manipulating the bits that make up the image. Here, you manipulate the instructions that make up the image. In the example with the image of a circle, you can make whatever you want with it. The limit is only the application that provides the tools for the manipulation. This is especially important when you manipulate parameters of an image over time.

Rasterization is the process of "rendering" or "flattening" a vector-based graphic to a bitmap graphic. This is often required during an export of a graphics file (so it can be viewed in other applications). In Motion this step is necessary at some point when working in 3D.

Shapes - Bezier - B-Spline

Shapes are defined by control points (x,y coordinates) and lines that connect those points. The connecting lines can be straight or curved based on math functions (Bezier curves, B-Spline). Connecting two points with a straight line creates a single line, three points create a triangle and so on. You can create shapes with as many points and connecting lines as you want. The shape can be open or closed depending on if you connect the last control point back to the first control point.

When creating shapes or manipulating them, keep in mind that the end result (and what the name of that particular shape is) depends on the selected parameter. Technically they are all the same just based on different mathematical models. For example, a circle shape has four control points connected with curved lines (Bezier curves). Changing the lines to straight lines results in a diamond shape with the same control points.

2D - 3D

In graphics application, of course everything is two dimensional. Any point is defined by its width (x) and hight (y) on a canvas. To create a 3D graphics just means that you use drawing techniques that gives the illusion of depth (z). In motion graphics this is even more effective by using moving object to create the illusion of a 3D space on a 2D screen.

Motion provides many great tools to create 3D motion graphics. Some extra rules apply in the 3D space versus the 2D space.

Filter

A filter is just a set of instructions applied to an object to alter its original appearance. Those alterations are mostly color changes but can include a wide variety of other visual effects.

Keyframe

Keyframes is a term used in video animation. Technically they are specific x,y coordinates in a mathematical function where x is a specific time value in your movie (represented by a specific frame) and y is the value of the parameter at that time (and a different value at a different time). Those "key" values represent "coordinates" or "nodes", i.e. the beginning and end value of a linear movement in an animation or a simple fade-in. The important part is that you only need a few keyframes because the values in between will be interpolated (calculated by the computer). Of course, the more complex the movements (changes of a parameter), the more keyframes are needed. I go into great details explaining the concept of Keyframes in my manual "Final Cut Pro X - The Details".

Motion Terms

Here are some of app specific terms used in Motion. This is just a short description to get an idea of what they are. Some of them belong to more advanced techniques that I cover later in this manual. However, I use them earlier in some chapters in the context of other topics, so this gives you a general idea what they are about.

 Project

A Project is what you are working on in Motion, your Composition. It contains all your material for that composition, the Objects (building blocks) and the instructions what to do with them.

 **Object**

Almost everything is in your Motion Project is an Object, mainly the building blocks of your Composition.

 **Generator**

A Generator is an Image Object that is a computer-generated graphic. Motion ships with a wide variety of Generators (shape based) and Text Generators (text based) ready to be used in your Project. Some are even built into the OSX system.

 **Behavior**

Behaviors are like modules that can be added to an Object like an effects plugin. Those Behaviors manipulate the Object over time based on physics simulations to create animation that would otherwise be way too complex to achieve with standard Keyframe animation.

 **Replicator**

This is an easy to use tool that creates kaleidoscopic patterns using any image object as the source material.

 **Particle Emitter**

This tool creates dynamic elements that change over time. Those elements, similar to the Replicator, are based on existing image objects that you assign the Particle Emitter to.

 **Camera - Light**

The Camera object and the Light object are used for creating 3D spaces. This is based on the concept that the appearance of each object in a 3D space is based on the position of the viewer (the camera) and any additional light source in relation to each individual object in your project.

 **Rig - Widget**

A Rig is an object that acts as a controller. You can build your own controllers in your Project containing so called widgets (sliders, checkboxes, menus) that are assigned to specific parameters or a range of parameters. This allows you to control a complex set of parameters with a single controller that functions like a macro control.

Objects

Virtually every element in your Project is an Object. There are different names for those objects and even different names for the same type of Object (besides calling them just elements, items or things). There are differences between Objects in regards to their functionality and interactivity with each other. Things can get complex very fast when the number of Objects in your Project grows. That's why it is a good idea to keep in mind to which category each Object belongs to and to know their individual behaviors. Here are the different categories of Objects, grouped by their functionality.

☻ Image Object (independent)

These are Objects that are visible in your Project that can function by themselves: Any kind of images, video clips, shapes, text, etc.

 Video   Image   Generator   Text   Shape   Shape (line)   Drop Zone

☻ Image Object (dependent)

These are Objects that are also visible in your Project but they cannot exist by themselves. They have to be attached to an Image Object to be visible. These are the different Masks, the Replicator and the Particle Emitter.

 Mask   Image Mask   Emitter   Replicator

☻ Effects Objects

These are Objects (Filters and Behaviors) that act as modules or plugins which can be added to almost every Object in a Project. They process or manipulate the object they are attached to.

 Filter   Behavior

☻ Control Objects

These Objects function as tools to control other objects, their parameters or complete sets of Objects/parameters. Rigs are general controllers, Camera and Light are special 3D tools.

 Rig   Camera   Light

☻ Other Objects

The Project Object represents your current Project.

A Group Object (2D) and   a Group Object (3D) act as containers for other objects. Their functionality is similar to a folder in the Finder.

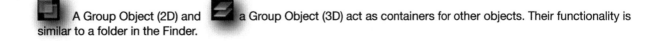 An Audio Object is not visible in your Composition but it is part of your Project if you want to add sound to your Project.

Another important aspect of Objects is the question of who is manipulating the Object.

Internal versus External

💡 Internal Control

You can build a simple motion-graphics project with just one Object. For example, a shape like a circle has so many parameters that you can manipulate over time with keyframes so you can create an animation of a bouncing ball. You can animate the movements as well as the deformation of the roundness when hitting the floor. Or change its color while flying. All those effects can be controlled "**internally**" within the one Object by manipulating the Object's own parameters.

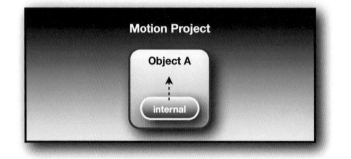

💡 External Control

The appearance of an Object can also be "controlled" externally just by the action of another Object, The final composition will be the result of interaction of the two Objects. In the example below ❶, even if you don't do anything to Object A, it will be affected externally by Object B. Placing Object B on top in the hierarchy of both Objects, then moving Object B across Object A will change its visibility. If Object B is a Mask in the shape of a binocular and Object A is a picture then just moving Object B will create a simple "spy effect" without touching Object A.

Of course, those external manipulations get more interesting when those (external) parameters are controlling the parameters of another Object ❷, kind of a "remote control".

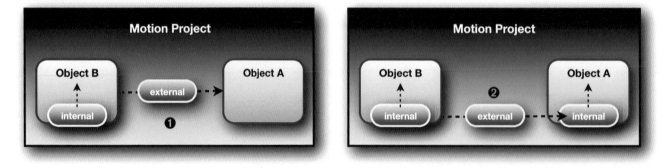

These were simple examples that include only two objects. Now multiply that to as many objects you might have in your Project with all the different internal and external manipulation and you have an idea why it is important to stay on top of what's going on with every object that you add to your project. On the other hand, if you stay on top of it, think about the power of such a system.

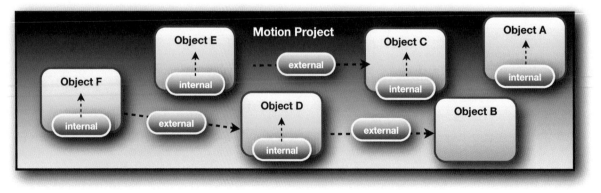

2 - Project

Before we learn "**HOW**" to work in Motion, we have to understand "**WHAT**" we are working on.

File Management

Most of the time, the topic of saving or exporting your file is covered more at the end of a manual. However, I want to introduce it here early on. The details of the File Management are often ignored altogether. After all, it is just the basic *new-save-open* routine of a typical application with maybe a few variations. I spent quite some time in my FCPx manuals explaining the underlying file mechanism of that program because a lot of confusion with that application is because of the misconception of WHAT the program is based on. In the case of FCPx, a database, a non document-based application.

Motion on the other hand is a document-based application. I think it is worth the time to review some basics in order to have a common understanding of document-based applications. We can then apply that to Motion to see where it complies or differs from common practice.

Like any other document-based application (i.e Word, Logic, ProTools), Motion follows the basic concept with its two main elements.

💡 **The Application**
The application is just the "shell", the environment that provides the interface and tools to create and work on whatever you are creating. These are applications known as "content-creation application" that enable you to create "something".

💡 **The Document**
And this is the "something" that you create in the application, the Document. For example, a book in Word, a music mix in ProTools, a song in Logic or a graphic in Photoshop.

Here is a diagram with the main elements of a document-based application like Motion.

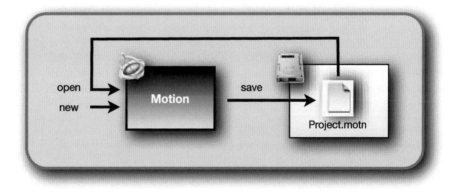

💡 **"Document" Name**
Some applications have a specific name for the document to better describe "what" it is you are working on. In Word it is just called a "Word Document", in Compressor it is a "Batch", in Logic it is a "Project". In Motion, you're also working on a "Project", or a "Motion Project".

💡 **New - Save - Open**
The first step after launching an application is to create a *New* document, you can *Save* that document to disk and *Open* that document later from disk to continue your work on it. The restriction that you could have only one Project open at a time and that you had to close an existing Project first before opening a new one was removed in version 5.0.5

💡 **File Extension**
Each Application uses their own file extension for the saved document. Some applications have more than one if they have different file formats (i.e. Word has .doc and .xdoc documents). A Motion document can have not one, not two, but four different kind of extensions. Definitely something to pay attention to. We'll get there in a moment.

💡 **File Location**
Some applications prefer that you store their documents in specific locations, but usually you can choose your own folder location. Motion also lets you pick your own location for your documents, but not for all! Read on.

Here are some additional features in document-based applications that are also used in Motion:

Template

This term is used to describe a document (Project) that has a specific purpose. Usually you work on a Project all the way to your final end result. But sometimes you might want to create Projects that you can use as a starting point. For example, in every letter that you write in Word, you have to set the format, write your name , address, enter your company logo, etc. At some point, it might be a good idea to create a document that just includes all that "redundant" work and save that as a Template. Now when you are about to write your next letter, you don't start from scratch, but use a copy of that Template that has all that pre-work already done for you. (another term for those files is "Stationaries").

Motion uses the concept of Templates too but here it uses it for a specific purpose, to create motion-graphics effects that can be used in FCPx. For example, you can create a complex transition effect in Motion that is made of different multiple effects or an elaborate Title sequence with 3D effects. Now instead of using that as a start for a specific work to create a final video for a client or a specific product, you save that Project as a Final Cut Template. Those templates can then be accessed by FCPx and used directly inside a FCPx Project.

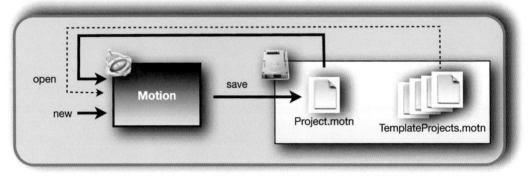

Export

This is another common element in content-creation applications. Usually, the file created by an application can only be read by the application itself. The document is in a proprietary file format for the purpose of creating the product (letter, mix, song, spreadsheet, etc). The file format however must often be converted to a different format once the work is done. For example, a ProTools project file that creates a music mix or a Logic project file cannot be played in iTunes. A FCP7 Project file cannot be played in the Quicktime player and a Photoshop file cannot be opened in iPhoto or Preview. Those documents have to be exported to a file format that the final "playback" application can read.
This procedure is often called an "Export" (or bounce), because you move it outside the realm of the application where it was created. The exported file is "flattened", meaning that you cannot change its individual elements anymore. Apple established the term "Share", found in the Main Menu of all of Apple's content-creation applications. Under that menu you find all the commands listed to export a document to a variety of different output formats. Other applications use the "Save as" command with the option to choose a different file format during the save procedure.

Motion also has the "Share" Menu that allows you to save a Motion Project in a file format that can be played by other applications, i.e. QuickTime, YouTube, Video Editing software, etc

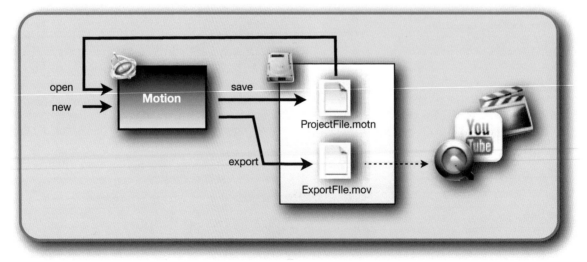

Publish

This term, coming from the printing world, implies that you make something available to a wider audience instead of keeping it for yourself.

In the case of Motion, saving a document file (a Project) is for the purpose of using it only in Motion itself. No other application is expected to read and use those special files anyway until you export them. However, as I mentioned earlier, FCPx uses Motion Projects for its Video Effects, Transitions, Titles and Generators. In order for FCPx to use those Motion Projects in its own application, it is necessary that those Motion Projects are located in a specific location for FCPx to "see". And that is what the Publish command in Motion is doing. It functions as a special save command that saves a Motion Project (a Motion Template to be specific) to a specific folder location, *"username/Movies/Motion Templates/"*.

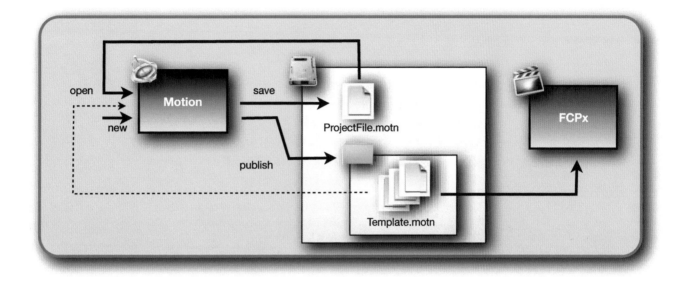

Now that we reviewed all the main elements of a document-based application regarding file management, let's put them into context and see how they work in Motion.

File Usage

As I mentioned in the previous chapter, a Motion Project can have two purposes:

- Create a standalone video file based on motion-graphics effects
- Create a Template for FCPx that uses motion-graphics effects

Create a standalone Video File

For this purpose, you use Motion as the application to create a final video. Instead of using FCP with video footage and effects, you can create a whole video within Motion if it is based mainly on motion-graphics elements instead of standard video clips. Of course, the final video that you create in Motion and export as a video file can again be imported later as a standard video clip as part of a bigger FCPx project, i.e. Main Title sequence, Animation sequence, Effects sequence, etc.

Under those circumstances, Motion behaves like a standard document-based application such as Photoshop or Word.

- ☑ You create a new Motion Project or open an existing Project (ProjectName.motn)
- ☑ You work on your document
- ☑ You save it as a Motion Project (ProjectName.motn) that contains all the individual elements
- ☑ Once the Project is ready, you export it as the final product, i.e. a Quicktime video file

Create a Template for FCPx

This is the other purpose for Motion Projects. Instead of working on a Motion Project to create a motion-graphics video for a specific job (i.e. a Title Sequence for a movie, a 3D animation for a commercial, etc), you can create motion-graphics Templates to use in FCPx. Of course, you could use those Templates also in Motion again to start a new Project.

FCPx already contains a wide variety of motion-graphics elements. They are available in the Media Browser in the form of four special types of Clips.

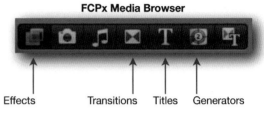

FCPx Media Browser

Effects   Transitions   Titles   Generators

- Effects
- Transitions
- Titles
- Generators

Those Clips are nothing other than Templates based on Motion Projects.

If you select any of the four buttons in the FCPx Media Browser, a window will display all those available Motion Templates for that type. It lists the built-in and user created Templates.

User created Templates

All the Templates that are stored in the location "*username/Movies/Motion Templates/*" will be listed in the FCPx Media Browser. These are the user-created Projects that you publish in Motion, or third-party Motion Effects that you installed on your machine. If you **ctr+click** on any Template in the FCPx Media Browser, a popup command "**Open in Motion**" lets you launch Motion and open that Template in case you wanted to edit it (you have to re-apply the effect again in FCPx if you edited and saved the Template in Motion).

Open in Motion

Built-in Templates

All the Motion Templates that come pre-installed with FCPx are stored in their own location, inside the FCPx application: "*/Applications/Final Cut Pro/Contents/PlugIns/MediaProviders/MotionEffect.fxp/Contents/Resources/Templates/*". You cannot edit those Templates directly. However, if you **ctr+click** on those Effects in the FCPx Media Browser, the popup command now reads "**Open a copy in Motion**". That means, FCPx copies that Template into the user created Template location first and opens that copy in Motion. The copy will show up right away in the FCPx Media Browser. (because it is in this dedicated folder that FCPx is reading)

Open a copy in Motion

FCPx - Effects Browser Window

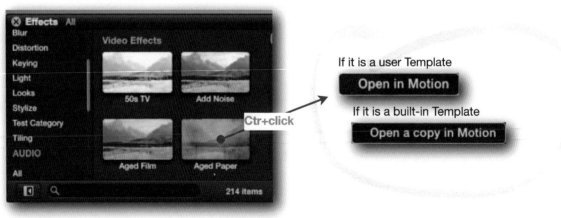

If it is a user Template

Open in Motion

If it is a built-in Template

Open a copy in Motion

Four Types of Motion Projects

There is one more aspect about Motion files to be aware of before actually starting with a Project.

As we just saw, a document-based application can save and open its documents (Projects) from its proprietary files. Those files usually have a unique file extension and file icon that identifies them. Most of those content-creation applications (ProTools, Logic, Photoshop, Word, Page, etc) have one file type. Motion however has four types of Project files with four different file extensions and four different file icons.

Generator	Effect	Transition	Title

.motn	.moef	.motr	.moti

It is very important to understand their purpose before starting with Motion. There are some subtle differences and overlapping functionalities that could cause confusion when you work with Motion Projects.

When you launch any content-creation application, you have basically two choices:

- Start from scratch with a new document (Project)

    This will be most likely the standard Main Menu command File ➤ New or Key Command cmd+N

- Open an existing document (Project) to continue working on it

    This will be most likely the standard Main Menu command File ➤ Open or Key Command cmd+O

Besides these two commands, an application might provide additional commands. But keep in mind, you start either from scratch or continue with an existing document. Even opening a Template is nothing more than opening an existing document.

Here are the choices in Motion's File Menu:

The commands for opening existing documents are standard:

- New: Create a new Project. This command depends on a setting in the Preferences ➤ Project window.
    - *Show Project Browser:* This opens the Project Browser window with a wide variety of options.
    - *Use Project "xyz":* This lets you define an existing Project that will open every time you use the *New* command.
- New From Project Browser... : This command has the same function as the first option in the previous Preferences setting. It opens the Project Browser window.
- The Open ... command with the dots hints that a standard File Selector Dialog will open to navigate to the existing Project file you want to open.
- The "Open Recent" command with a triangle for a submenu, standard in many applications, lists the recently opened Projects, so you don't have to navigate to them with the Open command.

So what we have here are two standard "New Project" commands and two "Open Project" commands. The Project Browser window provides many choices and settings options like a Swiss Army Knife for opening (new or exiting) Projects.

New / Open Template

The Project Browser window is divided into three main sections.

- On the left is a typical sidebar where you can make a selection.
- The middle section displays the content of the selected item in the sidebar. These are the actual Motion Projects.
- The section on the right provides the details of the selected Project in the center section.

Before going into the details about the Project Browser, I will focus first on why there are four Motion Projects.

For the moment, let's concentrate on only two selections in the sidebar:

❶ Blank: This is the actual "New" command. If you select "Blank" in the sidebar, 5 Motion Projects will be displayed in the middle section.

❷ This is where a "wait a minute" question could arise. I just explained that Motion has four different types of Motion Projects (based on the four file extensions), but now there are five to choose from. We recognize the four types "Effect", "Generator", "Transition" and "Title". Let's ignore the fifth one, "Motion Project", for a moment. Second question, why are they called "Final Cut Effect" and "Final Cut Transition" and not "Motion Effect" and "Motion Transition". It looks like you would create a new "Final Cut Effect" Project when you click on that icon and not a Motion Project.

I hope it is clear by now why these Motion Projects are labeled "Final Cut ...". Remember the second purpose for Motion, creating Motion Templates for FCPx. And this is exactly the case. Each of the four types of effects in FCPx (Effect, Transition, Title, Generator) is based on its own type of Motion Project, identifiable by its own extension and file icon.

If you want to create a new Motion Template for FCPx, this is where you start and choose which type of template specifically you want to create. Starting a Motion Project with any of those four new Templates will have one significant limitation later on. They can only be saved to the "*username/Movies/Motion Templates/*" location on your drive inside of one of four subfolders (one for each type) ❸. Now we understand why. This is the location where FCPx expects those files to be to make them available in the FCPx Media Browser. ❹

❺ These four items in the sidebar represent the four subfolders in "*username/Movies/Motion Templates/*". Selecting one item would display the Templates in that folder in the middle section of the Project Browser. This is like an "Open existing Template" command.

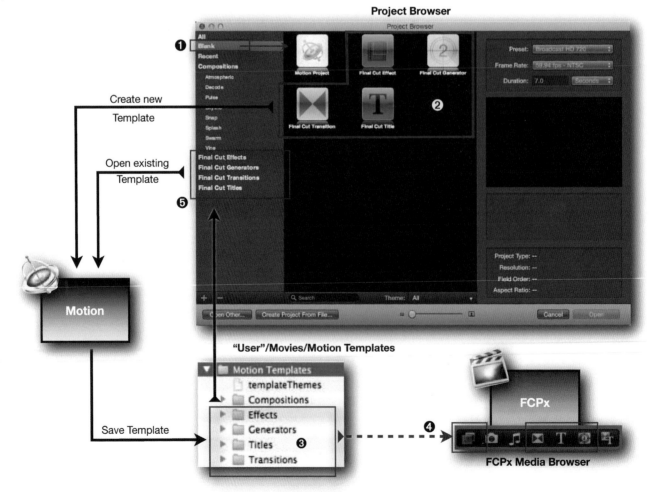

Project Browser

2 - Project

Save Template

Once you open a blank Template, Motion will create a new Motion Project with its standard user interface (see next chapter). There are two things that are special about those Template Projects:

- 🌐 A Template might have some basic elements/configuration that you cannot remove. This guarantees that you can only edit the Template to the degree that makes sense in the context of the selected type of Template. Other than that, the Motion interface is the same regardless which Template you are working on.

- 🌐 The *Save* and *Save As...* Command works as is typical in file management. However, it doesn't prompt a standard File Selector Dialog where you can navigate to a folder location. Instead, a special Sheet will slide out with the following settings:

  - ☑️ *Instructional text*: It includes what type of Template you are working on at the moment. The user interface itself doesn't give you any hint once you've started the Project. Only if you opened an existing Template, then the file extension in the window header would tell you what Project type is open at the moment.

  - ☑️ *Template Name*: Enter the name for the Template

  - ☑️ *Category*: You have to assign each Template to a Category. The popup menu initially provides only the item "New Category" first. This allows you to create new Categories that will be then available in the popup menu. A Category is nothing other than a subfolder inside each Template folder. This enforces a strict folder structure.

  - ☑️ *Theme*: You can assign an optional Theme to a Template. This can be used in the Project Browser to restrict the search for Templates that belong to a specific Theme. But it will also show up as a new Theme in the FCPx Theme Browser.

  - ☑️ *Include unused media*: If unchecked, only the media files (video audio, graphics) that are used in the Template will be saved.

  - ☑️ *Save Preview Movie*: This creates a little movie file of what the Project will look like. You can preview this in the Project Browser when you search for Templates.

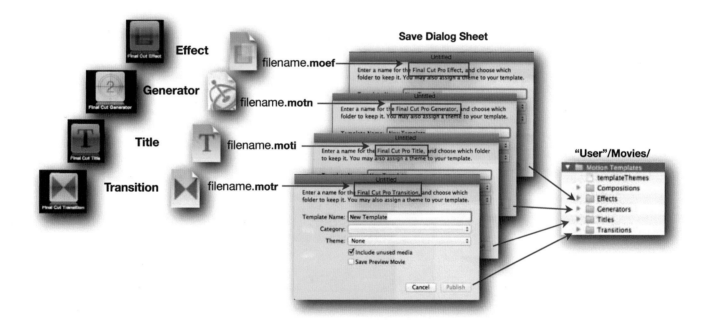

Please note two things:

- The window doesn't have a Save button. It is a "Publish" button. This is the right terminology. It is just inconsistent, because the File menu should list a "Publish" and "Publish As..." . That is what the command is doing, "publishing Templates".

- The Publish button is grayed out until you select a Category for the Template. This ensures that you don't save Templates on the top level of the Template folder.

Template Management

Let's have a look how the Motions Template folder is structured.

💡 Project Type Folder

These are the 4 main folders representing the 4 Final Cut Templates (Finder screenshot: red): "Effects, Generators, Transitions and Titles (I will discuss the "Compositions" folder in the next section),

💡 Category folder

In the screenshot of the Project Browser below, you can see two Categories that I created in the "Final Cut Effects" folder: "GEM-Test Category" and "GEM-Test2 Category" (You can *Add* or *Remove* Categories with the + and - button at the bottom of the sidebar ❶). You can see those Categories as Category folders with the same name in the Finder screenshot (orange).

💡 Template Folder

Inside the Category folder are the Templates, represented as their own folder (green), containing all the elements plus the actual Project File (grey).

💡 Theme Folder

If you've assign a Theme to a Template, then a folder with the Theme name (yellow) will be created inside the Category folder and the Template folder will now be placed in there.

At the bottom of the Project Browser is a Theme popup menu where you can restrict the displayed selection to only the Projects that have specific Themes assigned to them ❷. That popup menu also lets you create "New Themes..." and "Remove Theme" (the one that is currently selected).

Those Themes are stored in an xml file named "templateThemes" which is also located in the Motion Templates folder ❸ (after at least one Theme has been created).

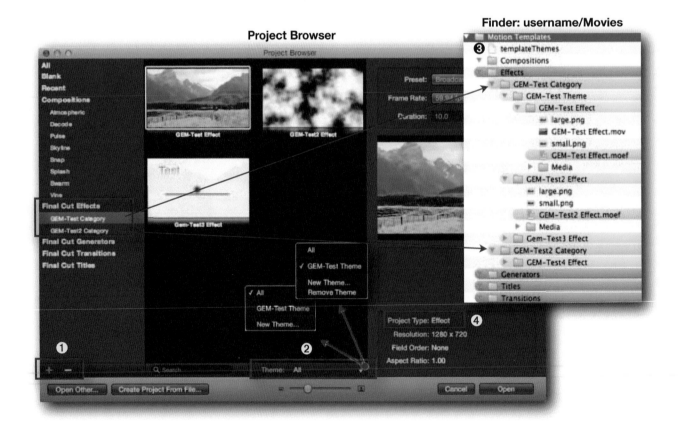

The right pane of the Project Browser displays a movie of the selected Project (if available) and underneath, the basic parameters of the Project, including the Project Type ❹.

FCPx Template Integration

Here is a look at how close the Motion Templates folder is integrated into FCPx:

- The Category folder inside the Motion Templates location will be represented in FCPx as a Category in the sidebar ❶ for each Template Type (Effect, Transition, Title, Generator).

- The Templates of the selected Category will be grouped by their assigned Theme ❷. Templates with no assigned Theme will be listed on top.

- When you select the Theme button ❸ from the Media Browser, FCPx lists on its sidebar all the Themes that were created in Motion for Final Cut Templates. Selecting a Theme in the sidebar will display all the Templates (of all types) that were assigned to that Theme ❹.

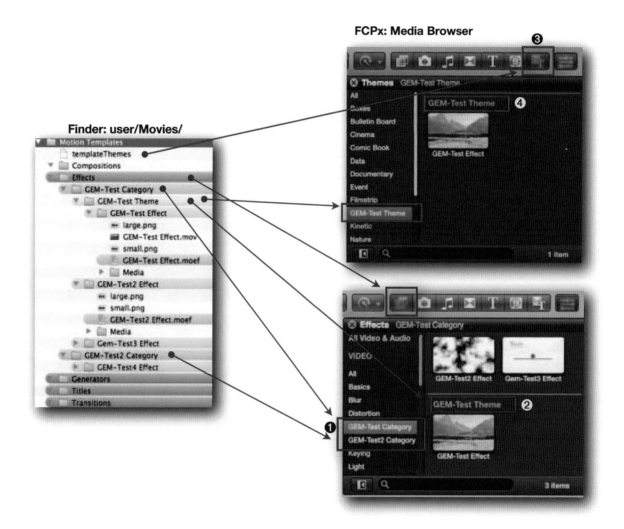

As I mentioned earlier, all the Final Cut Templates that are based on Motion (built-in or user created) can be opened directly from the FCPx Media Browser (right-click on the Template). However, any Final Cut Template that you edit in Motion, will not be updated if it was already placed on the FCPx Timeline. You have to replace it manually with the new Template.

The 5th Motion Project

I just explained the file management system regarding the four Project Templates that represent the four Project Types used in FCPx. However, there was a fifth Project Type in the Project Browser, "Motion Project". Does that mean we actually have five Project Types? The answer is, yes and no - you will see why.

In the previous chapter, where I asked the question "What is Motion for?", I listed two purposes:

- Create a standalone video
- Create a Template for FCPx

The second purpose should be clear by now. That's what the four Template Types are for. The fifth type, "Motion Project", is for the first purpose, "Create a standalone video", but also a little bit for the second purpose, "Create a Template". Since we've covered the functionality of Templates already, this potential confusion will be easier to understand.

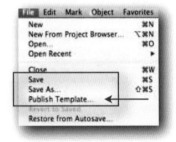

Once we select the "Motion Project" from the Project Browser, Motion will open a blank Project which looks pretty much the same as when we opened one of the other four Projects. However, there is one addition to the File Menu that the other Projects didn't have: **Publish Template ...**

Here is a diagram that shows what happens:

❶ The Save or Save As... command now allows you to save the Project to any location on your drive via a standard File Selector Dialog.

❷ The Publish Template... on the other hand behaves exactly as the Save command for any of the 4 Templates. A Dialog window opens that won't allow you to select a folder location. The location that the Template will be saved to, is restricted to the "Compositions" folder next to the other four Template folders inside the Motion Templates folder.

❸ The Publish Dialog gives you the additional option to save the Template as a Final Cut Generator.

❹ And here is the important part: All the options to save the Project to a file (Motion Project, Composition Template, Final Cut Generator) create a file with the same file extension (.**motn**) and the same file icon as Generators.

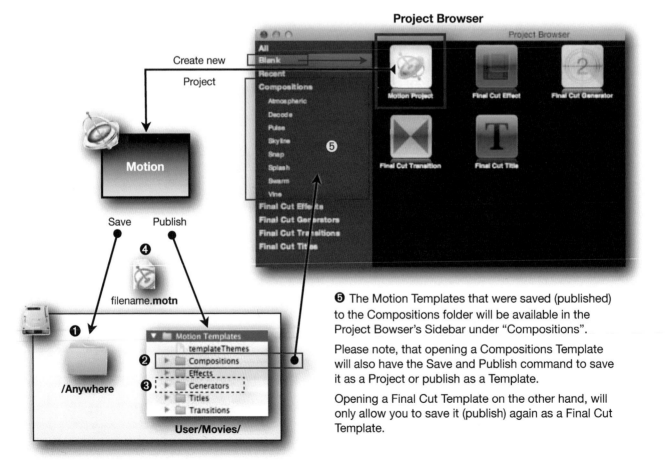

❺ The Motion Templates that were saved (published) to the Compositions folder will be available in the Project Bowser's Sidebar under "Compositions".

Please note, that opening a Compositions Template will also have the Save and Publish command to save it as a Project or publish as a Template.

Opening a Final Cut Template on the other hand, will only allow you to save it (publish) again as a Final Cut Template.

Here are the two screenshots of the Dialog window that opens when you select the "Save" or the "Publish Template" command:

💡 Save

The standard File Selector Dialog with an additional popup menu to choose if you want to copy any of the Project's media to the new location. The checkbox to "Include Unused Media" files is the same as with the Publish Dialog.

💡 Publish

The Publish Dialog is similar when saving Templates. The text indicates what type you are saving, a "Motion Composition". The last checkbox "Publish as Final Cut Generator" will save the Template as a Final Cut Generator to the Generators folder instead of the Motion Templates folder.

Compositions

When I explained the term Template, I defined it as a document that already includes some basic data. The four types of Final Cut Templates are a little special because the data prepared in them is to be used not in Motion but in a different app, FCPx. However, the Templates in the Compositions folder are actually Templates for Motion, Motion Projects that can be used as a starting point for Motion Projects (with the purpose of creating a standalone motion-graphics video).

The Project Browser displays only Final Cut Templates that you create yourself. That's why there are none when you select that type in the sidebar for the first time. However, not only does the Compositions section already include some Categories, but the Categories already include some Templates. These Templates are not found in the Compositions folder. They are embedded inside the Motion application (open from the Finders Shortcut Menu, "Show Package Contents"): */Applications/Motion/Contents/Templates/*

Here is a screenshot of that folder. The folder structure is the same as with the user's Motion Templates folder.

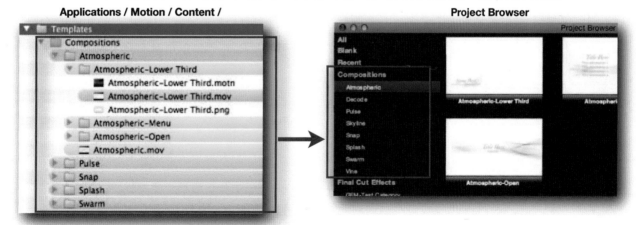

If you have Final Cut Pro 7 installed, then you might have additional Compositions Categories and Templates stored in the following location that also gets displayed in the Project Browser: */Library/Application Support/Final Cut Pro/Templates/ Compositions/*. Please note that the Templates that are saved from Motion are only available in FCPx to the same logged-in user on that specific machine. Copying Templates to that System Library location makes the Templates accessible to all users (Check out the third party app "*Motion Template Tool*")

Project Overview

Here is the final overview regarding the question of whether or not there are four or five Motion Projects:

💡 There are 5 Project types

> The Project Browser displays the "Project Type" in the right lower corner for the selected Project or Project Template

💡 There are 4 Project file types

> Motion uses 4 unique file extensions and file icons. Please note, that a Motion Project, a Composition template and a Final Cut Generator template use the same file extension and file icon.

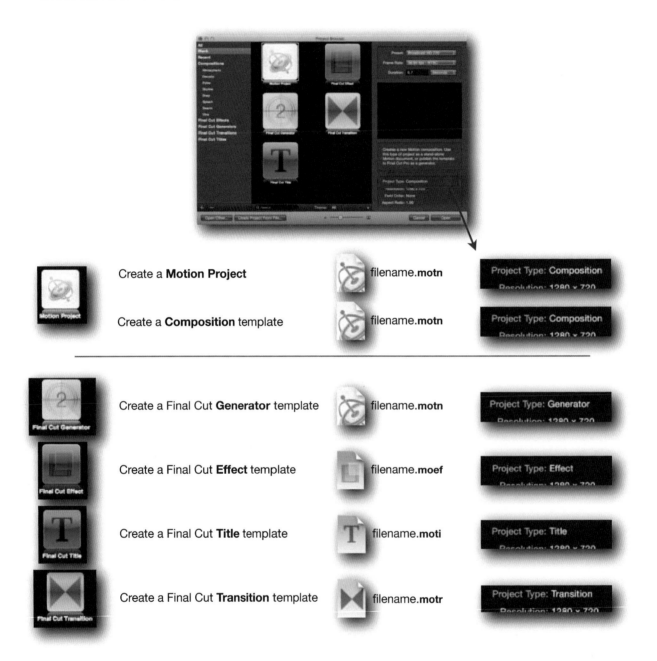

Unlike with FCPx, Motion files are allowed to be moved around in the Finder (or exchanged with other users). If a Motion file exists outside the Motion Templates folder, it still can detect which Project type it is by its file extension. The exception however is a .motn file, which has three possibilities. If it is located in the Generators folder, then it opens as a Final Cut Generator template, if it is in the Compositions folder then it opens as Compositions template. If it is located anywhere else, then it opens a s Motion Project.

Other Project Settings

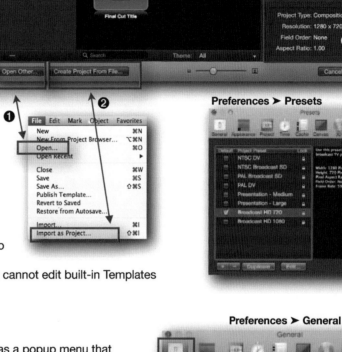

💡 Project Browser

❶ The "*Open Other...*" button functions the same as the "Open" command from the File menu.

❷ The "*Create Project From File ...*" button functions the same as the "*Import as Project ...*" command from the File menu. It creates a new Project with the currently selected Media files.

❸ The info pane in the lower right corner lists the parameters of the selected Project (including the Project type).

❹ The settings in the upper right corner is only active for new (blank) Projects. They set the parameters for the new Project. Those parameters can be changed later with the exception of the Frame Rate.

❺ The Preset popup menu can be edited in the Preferences ➤ Presets window. That's where you can create your own Presets and select the default Preset.

❻ Please note, the "*Open*" button switches to "*Open a Copy*" when you select a built-in Template from the Compositions section (you cannot edit built-in Templates directly).

Preferences ➤ Presets

💡 At Startup

The General tab in the Preferences window has a popup menu that determines the behavior during the launch of Motion.

- 💡 *Open Last Project*: Opens the last Project that you worked on.

- 💡 *Create New Project*: This behavior depends on another setting: Preferences ➤ Project ➤ "For New Documents"

  - *Show Project Browser*: This will open the Project Browser

  - *Use Project ...*: The *Choose ...* button lets you define any of your Templates. This one will then open up when you launch Motion the next time

Preferences ➤ General

Preferences ➤ Project

💡 Autosave

The Cache tab in the Preferences window provides detailed settings for the Autosave behavior.

Also, the File Menu includes a "Restore from Autosave ..." command to access any of the autosaved versions of the Project.

Please note that Motion does not support "Versioning" under OSX 10.7 (Lion). Versioning is the new concept for saving files that many of Apple's applications use. It eliminates the need for manually saving a document file which is saved automatically. This is done invisibly at the system level.

Preferences ➤ Cache

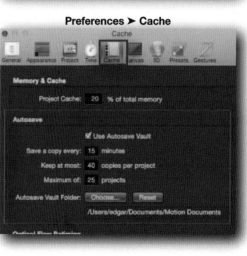

3 - Interface

Concept

Here is a simple diagram with 7 elements in Motion that describe its basic concept:

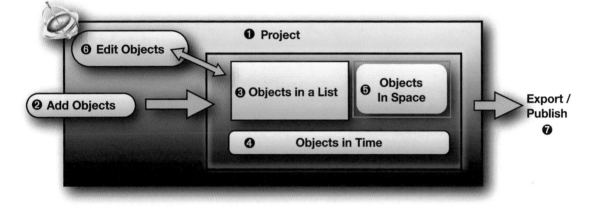

The first two elements are the most important ones:

❶ Project

This is the environment where you create your current work, the Project, your Composition. It is represented by the user interface that provides all the necessary elements (windows, tools, menus, etc). The two main parameters of the Project are its length (duration) and its frame size (width x height). These are the same parameters as a video file because that is what you are creating and exporting at the end - a video file (except when creating Templates).

❷ Object

An Object is the other important element. They are the building blocks of your Project (shapes, text, images, videos, etc). It is the material (design elements) that you bring into your Project or create from scratch inside the Project.

The next three elements have basically the same purpose. They let you look at the Objects that are currently in your Project. They just provide a different "view", a different way to look at the same Objects (and edit them in that context).

❸ Objects in a List (Project Pane)

All the available Objects are arranged in a list. It is like a stack that represents the hierarchy of the Objects from top to bottom. The top (graphical) object covers the next object underneath, and so on (if they are placed in the same space).

❹ Objects in Space (Canvas)

This is the area where you view and edit the same objects in space (2D or 3D). Your space is represented by the size of the frame where you can arrange the Objects. The frame size is one of the main parameter of your Project.

❺ Objects in Time (Timing Pane)

In this window element, you decide the timing information for each Object. When is the Object visible and when not during the duration of the Project. In addition to that, virtually every parameter of an Object can be changed over the duration of the Project (animated) providing complete control of the Object's appearance over time.

Each Object in a Project can be manipulated by editing any of its available parameters:

❻ Edit Object

Various windows display the parameters of a selected Object for viewing and editing.

After the editing is done and the Project is finished, it can be exported as a Video or published as a Template:

❼ Export / Publish

Now let's see how those basic elements of the Motion concept are laid out in the Motion interface. A few technicalities first:

- Motion has a single window interface. All the elements (window panes) that can be displayed or hidden are connected as part of one big window. Although it restricts the creation of custom window layouts, it helps to focus when working in Motion because the main elements are always in the same location (left, right, down up, etc)
- There are only a few small free floating windows besides the main window.
- The restriction that you can have only one Project open at a time was removed in version 5.0.5.

This is the elegant part of the GUI:

The three sections to "view" the Objects in your Project are nicely arranged in the interface.

- The "Objects in Space" view is placed at the top right and is called the **Canvas.**
- The "Object in a List" view is located to its left and is called the **Project Pane**.
- The "Objects in Time" view is located below those two elements and is called the **Timing Pane.**
- Between those three window panes is a strip that provides the tools to work on those Objects, the **Toolbar**.

And here is the not so elegant part of the GUI:

The other two elements, "Add Objects" and "Edit Objects" of the Motion concept, have to share the same space in the user interface (window pane), which is not as elegant from a logical point of view.

- In comparison, the Project Pane (Objects in a List) has three tabs which display a variation of that specific view. The name of that pane (Project Pane) still makes sense regardless of which tab is selected.
- Now the window pane on the left also has three tabs. However, one tab, *Inspector*, belongs to the element "Editing Objects" (the Objects that are in your existing Project) and the other two tabs, *File Browser* and *Library*, belong to the element "Add Objects" which is for Objects that are not in your Project.
- The Inspector is one of the most important GUI elements in any content-creation application and in virtually all of those apps provide either a separate window pane or a floating window(s) for the Inspector.

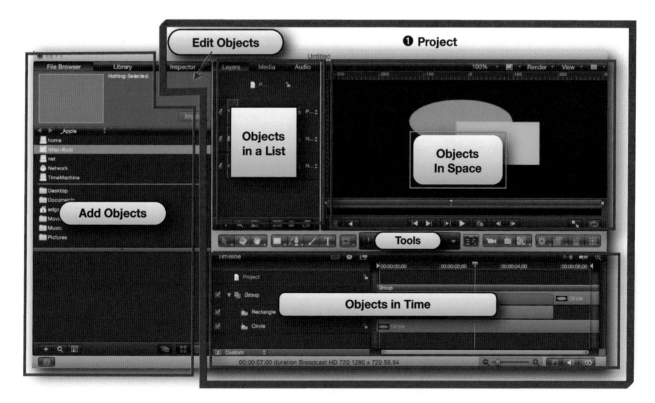

The big border that I drew indicates how I would mark the interface from a logical point of view: The sections that deal with stuff in your Project and the sections that deal with the stuff outside the Project, resources that can be brought into the Project. That little corner around the Inspector indicates the little imperfection of the GUI, because I consider the Inspector part of the Project.

Window Panes

Now let's have a look just at the mechanics of the various window sections (panes).

💡 1 Canvas

The Canvas is the main window pane that is always visible. After all, this is where you can view your Composition the way it will look when you export it. This window cannot be hidden. Quite the opposite. The "Full Screen" button (1a) lets you hide all the other currently visible window panes. This button toggle between those two states and is also available as the Key Command F8 or from the Main Menu Window ➤ Player Mode. There is a little inconsistency with the terminology. The tool tip window displays "Full Screen" for the function of the button but the Main Menu calls this command "Player Mode". Please note that the term Full Screen refers here to the full Project window, not the full screen of the computer display.

💡 2 Project Pane

This window section is positioned in the center of the GUI and shares its space with the Canvas. This means that only the canvas will resize itself when toggling this pane. The other two window panes are not affected. The Project Pane can be toggled with the button on the left lower corner of the Canvas (2a). Same function as the Key Command F5 or Menu Command Window ➤ Show/Hide Project Pane. Each of the three views also have their own Key Command to switch between them (cmd+4, cmd+5, cmd+6). Using a command for a view that is already visible, will then hide the whole pane.

💡 3 Timing Pane

This window section below the Canvas can display three different Timelines. They can be shown or hidden individually with the three buttons at the lower right corner (3a) and resize automatically to share the available size of this window pane. Each of the three buttons (views) also has its own Key Command to toggle it (cmd+7, cmd+8, cmd+9). If none of the Timelines is shown then the Timing pane will disappear and let the Canvas (plus Project Pane) take over the space. You can show or hide the Timing Pane with the Key Command F6 or Menu Command Window ➤ Show/Hide Timing Pane. The current selection of the three individual Timelines is remembered when toggling this way.

💡 4 "File Browser, Library, Inspector" Pane

This pane (without a specific name) can be shown or hidden with the button in the lower left corner (4a). I pointed out already that this section with its three different views is not all logical from a user interface point of view. Using an "I" button is also questionable because this is normally used for an "Inspector" window. Here, it switches the whole pane, not only the Inspector. Also, this pane doesn't have its separate Key Command like the Project Pane and Timing Pane (maybe because it doesn't have its own name). Each of the three views however has its own Key Command to switch between them (cmd+1, cmd+2, cmd+3). Using a command for a view that is already visible, will then hide the whole pane.

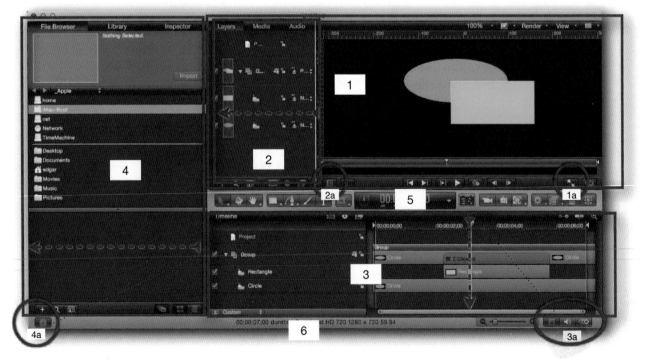

Of course, all the various panes (1-4) can be resized by dragging their divider line between them.

There are two more sections of the Motion Window that are not window panes. They play an important role because they are always visible:

5 Toolbar

This strip is located below the Canvas and has a similar function as the "*Toolbar*" in FCPx. It contains all the various tools you need when working in Motion. Those tools are arranged in groups of buttons, most of them containing their own popup menus. The Toolbar also contains the Time Display in the center.

6 Status Bar

This section at the very bottom actually belongs to the whole window frame. The center displays the properties of your current Motion Project (Length, Format, Resolution and Frame Rate). It also contains on the left the button to toggle the left "NoName" pane (4a) and on the right the buttons (3a) to toggle the three views of the Timing Pane. (and a zoom slider for the timeline).

If you have a quick look at the four buttons that toggle the window panes (1a, 2a, 3a, 4a), then you realize that they are all located on those 'always visible' window elements.

And here is the Project window again with the various controls and Key Commands.

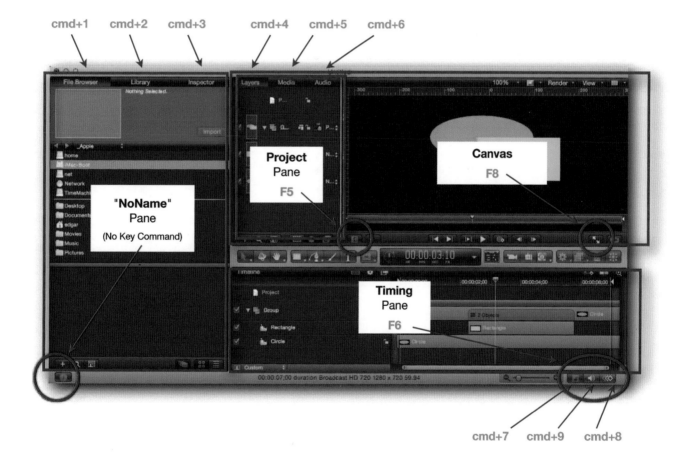

Another example of an almost perfect (logical) user interface. All the tabs/sections of the window panes have a logical order in how the Key Commands are assigned to them. Command Key plus Number 1 to 9 for the tabs from left to right. Oops, the number 8 and 9 are out of order (I said almost perfect).

Inspector vs HUD

Most of the content-creation applications use the concept of an Inspector. This is a special window that displays its content depending on the selected object(s) in a different window. (I go into great details about that concept in my manual "Compressor 4 - How it Works")

Let's look at the difference between the actual data and the metadata (data about data) of an object. A few examples:

- ◉ If you change the text in your word document, you change the actual data. Changing the font or any other formatting, hanges the metadata of the text.
- ◉ If you replace a clip in the FCPx timeline, you change the actual data. Applying any effect to a clip or adding notes to it is considered changing its metadata.
- ◉ If you add an image to your Motion Project, then the image itself can be considered the data. Any manipulation of that image in any form or shape is considered changing its metadata.

All that metadata is usually displayed in a separate Inspector window. Most of Apple's applications implement the Inspector window as a floating window which is always on top of any other window (e.g., Pages, Numbers, Keynote, etc). Sometimes you can even open multiple Inspector windows to have as many parameters accessible as possible at a time. In FCPx, the Inspector is part of its single window interface as a window pane that can be shown or hidden but doesn't float.

Motion uses both interface concepts:

- ☑ Inspector as an integrated window pane
- ☑ Inspector as a free floating window - the HUD

HUD - Heads Up Display

In addition to having an Inspector as a fixed window pane, Motion provides the HUD (Heads Up Display) which is nothing other than an additional floating Inspector window (The Inspector's *Mini-Me*). The HUD displays a subset of all the data that is displayed in the Inspector pane. Although an exception to the single window interface concept, the HUD gives you more flexibility to access often used data quickly without switching window panes. The little window (which can't be resized) is also semi transparent, so you can see elements underneath even if they are covered by the HUD.

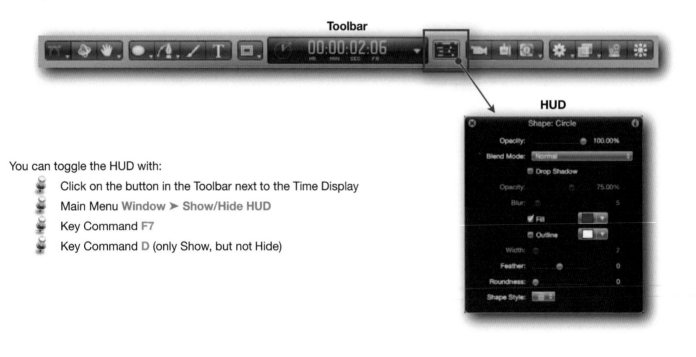

You can toggle the HUD with:

- ◉ Click on the button in the Toolbar next to the Time Display
- ◉ Main Menu Window ➤ Show/Hide HUD
- ◉ Key Command F7
- ◉ Key Command D (only Show, but not Hide)

Here is the concept:

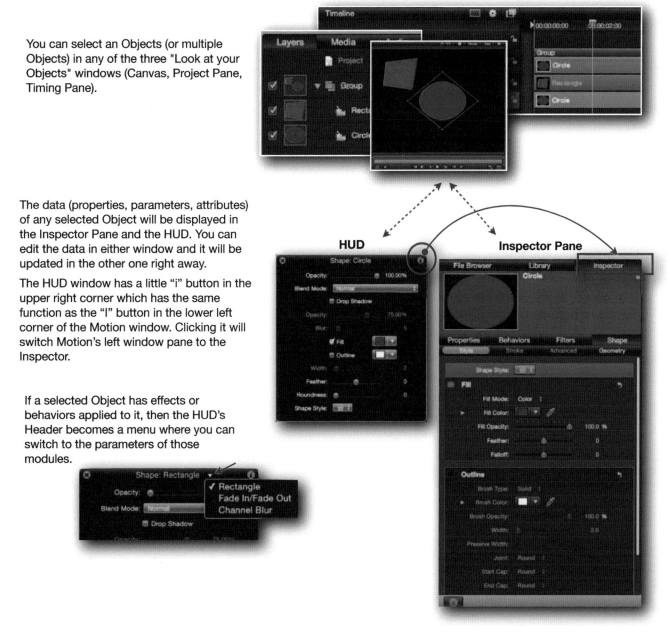

Canvas, Project Pane, Timing Pane

You can select an Objects (or multiple Objects) in any of the three "Look at your Objects" windows (Canvas, Project Pane, Timing Pane).

The data (properties, parameters, attributes) of any selected Object will be displayed in the Inspector Pane and the HUD. You can edit the data in either window and it will be updated in the other one right away.

The HUD window has a little "i" button in the upper right corner which has the same function as the "I" button in the lower left corner of the Motion window. Clicking it will switch Motion's left window pane to the Inspector.

If a selected Object has effects or behaviors applied to it, then the HUD's Header becomes a menu where you can switch to the parameters of those modules.

HUD

Inspector Pane

Edit Tools

The HUD has a special function that the Inspector doesn't have. It can edit Tools. For example, if you select the Rectangle Tool from the Toolbar to draw a Rectangle Object (discussed in a later chapter), then the question is: What default attributes will the rectangle have?

HUD

Tool selected

And this is exactly what you can set in the HUD.

If you select a Tool and no Object is selected (which has priority over Tools), then the HUD displays those default parameters. Now you can set those parameters before you actually create the object, instead of creating the object first and changing the parameters afterwards (which you still can do). The window header of the HUD indicates what it is displaying at the moment, the "type of the Object" or the "type of the Tool".

Once you created an Object, the HUD will switch automatically from Tool display to Object display, because the Object is automatically selected after you created it.

Inspector

The Inspector window has 3 sections:

💡 *Preview/Info*: At the top is the Preview/Info section which displays a thumbnail and next to it the general info about the selected Object (mostly for media files). The Preview thumbnail is linked to the Playhead. Whatever shape or form the Object has at the time position the playhead is parked on, that will be displayed in the thumbnail.

💡 *Modules*: All the parameters are grouped in Modules instead of displaying them all in one long endless list.

💡 *4 Tabs*: All those Modules are again grouped. They are available in those tabs:

- **Properties**: This tab contains basic Parameters that are available for most Objects (Transform, Blending, Crop, Timing, etc)

- **Behaviors**: Any Behavior Object that is assigned to this Object will be displayed as a Module in the Behaviors tab.

- **Filters**: Any Filter Object that is assigned to this Object will be displayed as a Module in the Filters tab.

- **"Object"**: This is called the Object tab and the tab is labeled "Object" if no Object is selected. When you select an Object, then this tab will be labeled with the type of the Object, like *Shape, Text, Mask*, etc. Even the Project itself is an Object and displays its parameters when selected in the Project Pane. This tab contains all the modules that define the default parameters of an Object.

  - **Sub-Tabs**: Four types of Objects (Project, Shape, Text, Text Generator) have their modules organized in subgroups. They are displayed as additional tabs below the four main tabs.

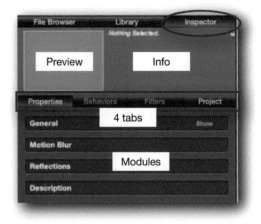

Objects with extra sub-tabs

Many interface elements in the Inspector are similar to FCPx. As a FCPx user, this will make you feel home right away:

❶ Modules can be expanded or collapsed with the blue Show/Hide command (when mouse over) or by a **double+click** on the header.

❷ The module contains the various controls, buttons and menus to modify the Object. Some Parameters have their own disclosure triangle to reveal even more parameters (Compound Parameters, Sub-Parameter).

❸ The Reset button reverts to the module's default settings.

❹ Individual parameters display the Keyframe buttons when moused over.

❺ On the right is the Animation popup menu. It is available for the header and for the parameters. This menu has two extra menu items, "Add to Rig" and "Add Parameter Behavior".

❻ Some Modules can be bypassed with the blue on/off button on the header.

❼ The pad lock button in the upper right corner locks the Inspector to its current view. This lets you switch to different Objects without having the Inspector following the selection.

Inspector Controls

Here is an overview of the different controls and their functionality in the Inspector. The module has to be enabled in order to make changes to the enclosed parameters.

- **Value Box:** This is a numeric value that can be changed by double clicking on it and typing a new value or dragging the value up and down. This functionality is called a value slider which is indicated by a small arrow above and below the number.

  Pay attention when the number is red. This indicates the "Initial Keyframe Method" which I explain the Timing Pane chapter.

- **Slider:** You can drag the slider or click on the slider line to jump to that value. Opt+click on the slider line will change the value by plus or minus 1.

  - Pay attention to the slider knob with a black dot on it. This means that this is a slider group, where its individual slider value has offsets.

  - Sliders are limited to a maximum value (i.e. 100), even if the parameter can be set to a much higher value with the value box or the onscreen controls in the Canvas.

  This is an example of a so called "Compound Parameter". It is a controller (slider, knob, value, etc) that controls multiple sub-Parameters at the same time. The sub-Parameters can be revealed with the disclosure triangle to adjust them separately.

- **Dial:** just drag the dial left-right or up-down.

- **Checkboxes, Menus:** they behave as expected.

- **Text info, Text entry:** A few modules have read only text information (Media Object) or text boxes to enter descriptions (Project Properties).

- **Source Well:** These is a little square area that lets you drag an objects onto it. The module uses it as source material for various processing. Drag the item out of the well to empty it.

- **Color Well:** This is a control area for selecting colors. It has three elements.

  - The *Color Swatch* opens the floating Colors Window: This is the standard OSX Colors Window with all its functionality.

  - The arrow opens the popup Color Palette: This is a quick in-and-out popup window that lets you pick a color by moving the mouse (shape of a eyedropper) over the available color spectrum. When clicked on, the color is set and the window disappears.

  - Eyedropper: Clicking on this icon changes the cursor to an eyedropper that lets you click on any area in the Canvas to pick that color. Once clicked on an area, it resets to the regular cursor again.

    Color Slider: Opening the color parameter with its disclosure triangle, reveals three sliders and value boxes to set the RGB values separately.

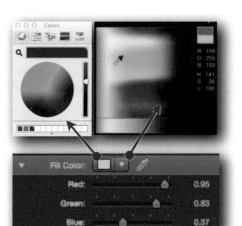

- **Gradient Editor:** The Gradient Editor uses the various color controls plus some additional ones to set the color, color position, number of colors, opacity, direction, and interpolation of a gradient.

- **Drag-and-drop Parameter value:** You can drag a whole parameter row over to another parameter (in the same module) to copy its value(s). You will see a little shadow of the original parameter section while you're dragging the mouse which changes to a green plus sign to indicate the copy-paste action.

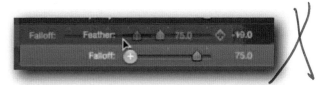

4 - Adding Objects

Now that we have a basic idea what a Motion Project is and what the basic interface elements are, let's start with the elements needed to create a Project, the building blocks or *Objects*.

Add Objects

When starting with a blank Project (not a Template), nothing is in there. It is blank, empty. So the first step would be to add Objects to build the Project. Please keep in mind that almost every "thing" in Motion is called an Object. In this context however, we'll talk about the Objects that are the main building blocks of a Motion Project.

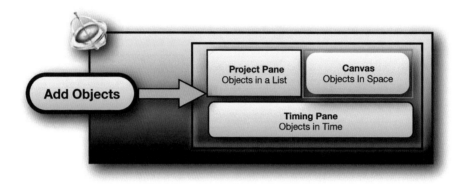

There are two ways to add new Objects to your Project:

💡 **Adding Existing Objects**

> These are elements (files) that already exist outside your current Project. You can divide them in two groups:
>
> - Media files: video, images, audio.
> - Computer-generated Graphics: any vector-based file, mainly from Motion or available from the OSX system.

💡 **Create New Objects**

> These are the Objects that you create from scratch in your Motion Project.

Object Types

I introduced the different types of Objects in the first chapter and grouped them based on their similar functionality inside a Motion Project. Always be aware what a specific Object can do or what you can do with that Object. We will get into that step by step.

Resources

So between the newly created and the existing Objects, lets look at the existing Objects first and see how to add them to the Project.

There are three sources from which you can add Objects.

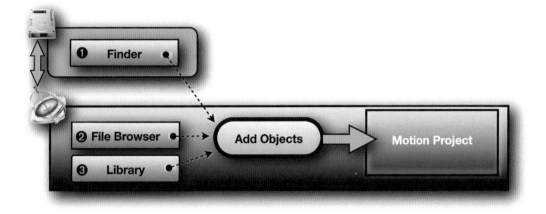

❶ From the Finder

This is the simple drag-and-drop procedure where you drag a file directly from a Finder window onto the Motion window. You can drag it onto either one of the three window panes that represent your Motion Project: Canvas, Project Pane, Timing Pane.

❷ From the File Browser

The File Browser is one of the three views on the left window pane in Motion (the window pane that doesn't have a name). This window functions like a mini-Finder built into the Motion interface, where you can browse and select media files that are available on your mounted drives.

❸ From the Library

The Library is the second of the three views in that window pane. This window provides an interface to browse, manage and select Objects that ship with Motion and Objects that you created yourself (plus a few other types of Objects that are explained below).

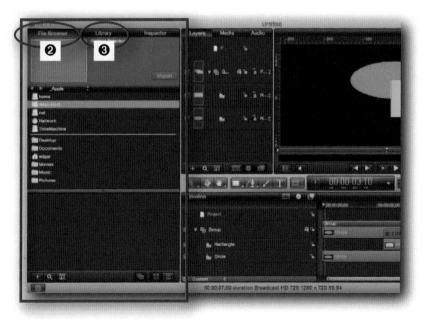

Let's have a closer look at those two windows.

File Browser

You can toggle the File Browser window with any of these commands:

- Main Menu **Window ➤ File Browser**
- Key Command **cmd+1**
- Click the "i" button in the lower left corner to show/hide the left window pane
- Click on the "File Browser" tab in the left window pane (if visible)

The File Browser window is divided into three main sections plus some additional controls:

❶ The center section, called the "**Sidebar**", displays two areas separated by a horizontal divider line. The upper portion displays all the mounted and networked volumes (the top level of your computer) and the lower portion displays the top level of your home folder.

❷ The lower section of the File Browser, called the "**Stack**" displays the content of the folder (or drive) that is selected in the Sidebar. Here you can select a file or click on any folder to navigate deeper into the file structure.

❸ The file path is displayed in the Path popup menu above the Sidebar. Here you can also step up in the file hierarchy by selecting any of the levels from the popup menu. The left and right arrow next to the popup menu are the "*Browse History*" buttons. They work the same as in the Finder (or in FCPx for the Project History) and go to the previous or next viewed file/folder. Those buttons support the three-finger-swipe on a Trackpad.

❹ The top section of the File Browser is the "**Preview**" that shows or plays the file that is selected in the Stack. You can set in the Preferences whether or not the file starts playing immediately when selected.

❺ Manage Files:
Because the File Browser is just an alternative to the Finder, you can do some file management right here.

- Rename a file by selecting "Rename" from the Shortcut Menu or selecting a file, hit return and enter the name.

- Create a new folder with the plus button at the bottom of the File Browser.

- Delete a file or folder by selecting "Move to Trash" from the Shortcut Menu.

- You can even drag a file from your Project back onto the Stack. This will copy that file to the Finder.

- Search for specific files with the magnifying glass which opens a search box.

❻ Import Files:

You can Import the selected file (or multiple files) into your Project in two ways:

- Drag it directly from the Stack to any of the three panes of your Project (Canvas, Project Pane, Timing Pane)

- Click the import button in the Preview area.

Name and information about the selected file

Mute audio

Click to import the selected file to the Project

❹ Preview

❻

❸ Navigation Controls

File Path menu:
It displays the file path to the currently selected file

❶ Sidebar

ctr+click on a file in the Stack to open the Shortcut Menu

❷ Stack

Open in Viewer
Open in QuickTime Player
Reveal in Finder
Rename
Move to Trash

❺

Display the Stack in Icon View or List View

Create new folder

❺

Search for specific files

Resize slider for Icons in Icon View (or use 2-finger pinch on a trackpad)

"Show Image Sequence as collapsed" button lets you import an image sequence as a single object

Library

You can toggle the Library window with any of these commands:

- Main Menu Window ➤ Library
- Key Command cmd+2
- Click the "i" button in the lower left corner to show/hide the left window pane
- Click on the "Library" tab in the left window pane (if visible)

The Library window is similar to the File Browser. Let's look at those elements first before introducing the Library details.

❶ The center section, again called the "**Sidebar**", works a little bit different than in the File Browser. Here you have two columns. The left column lists the Categories all the available Objects are organized in. Selecting any of those categories will display a folder with the subcategories in the right column.

❷ The lower section of the Library, also called the "**Stack**", displays the content of the subcategory folder that is selected in the right column of the Sidebar above. It displays the Objects or one more subfolder level.

❸ The file path of the selected item in the Stack is displayed in the Path popup menu above the Sidebar. You can also use it to navigate the file hierarchy. The left-right arrows next to the popup menu are the "*Browse History*" buttons. Those buttons support the three-finger-swipe on a Trackpad. In that same section is a "Theme" popup menu that I describe below.

❹ The top section of the File Browser is the "**Preview**" which shows or plays the Object that is selected in the bottom section, the Stack. You can set in the Preferences whether or not the file starts playing immediately when selected.

❺ Managing Objects:

There are similar commands but the Library has a few more specifics that I describe on the next page. Here is an overview:

- Rename Objects is only possible for Objects that are placed in the Library by the user (Custom Objects).

- Create a new folder in the selected Stack or the selected Sidebar (right column) with the Plus button.

- Delete a (user created) Custom Object or folder with the Main Menu Command Edit ➤ Delete.

- You can also drag an Object from your Project back to the Library.

- Search for specific Objects with the magnifying glass which opens a search box.

❻ Apply Object:

Instead of importing a file, here you "Apply" an Object to your Project. This term makes sense when the selected Object manipulates another Object (filter, effect, style, etc). If it is an Image Object (Shape, Generator, etc) then you technically "import" that Object to your Project. You can do this in two ways:

- Drag the Object directly from the Stack to any of the three panes of your Project (Canvas, Project Pane, Timing Pane)

- Click the Apply button in the Preview area.

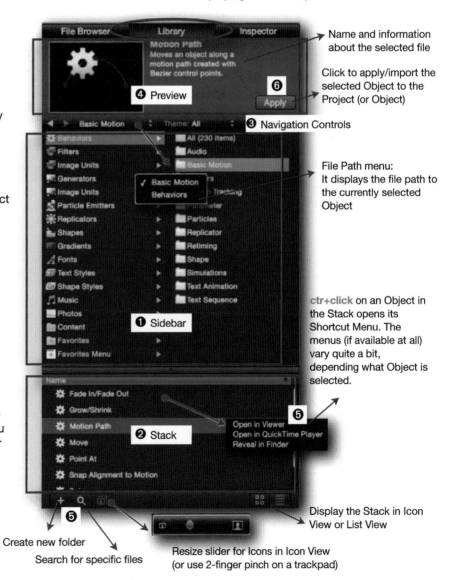

Name and information about the selected file

Click to apply/import the selected Object to the Project (or Object)

❸ Navigation Controls

File Path menu: It displays the file path to the currently selected Object

ctr+click on an Object in the Stack opens its Shortcut Menu. The menus (if available at all) vary quite a bit, depending what Object is selected.

Display the Stack in Icon View or List View

Create new folder

Search for specific files

Resize slider for Icons in Icon View (or use 2-finger pinch on a trackpad)

Library Content

Let's have a closer look at the left column of the Sidebar to see what Object Categories are available. I like to re-arrange them based on the types of Objects I introduced in the Introduction Chapter of this book.

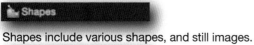

Library Content

💡 **Image Objects (independent)**

Generators are computer-generated graphics (stills or motion graphics). Image Units are additional Generators that are built into OSX as part of the Core Image technology (starting with OS X 10.5)

Shapes include various shapes, and still images.

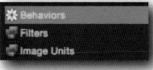

These media files can also be accessed from the File Browser window. However, the Library window provides a better interface, listing all of the playlists for your iTunes Library and the albums in your iPhoto Library. (Of course, music files don't belong to the Image Objects, but I kept them together as media files)

💡 **Image Objects (dependent)**

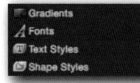

These are the "visible" Image Objects that need to be assigned to another Object. However, these Objects from the Library already come with an Image Object that they are applied to so it can be added to the Project as an independent Image Object.

💡 **Effect Objects**

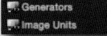

These are all the Effects Objects provided by Motion that get assigned to other Objects and function like effects plugins. Image Units (same name as Generator Image Units, but different icon) are the Filters that are built into OSX as part of the Core Image technology (starting with OS X 10.5).

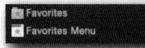

These four categories are not actually Objects. They act more as presets, changing the parameters of the Objects they're applied to in order to achieve a specific effect. Therefore they won't show up as individual Objects in your Project.

💡 All the above

This folder is a huge collection of all kinds of Objects, even media files, that come with Motion.

💡 Others

You can place any Objects to these custom folders for quick access of your favorite or often used Objects. See the next page for details.

Custom Content

The Library pane acts as an interface to the actual location of the Objects on your local drive. With the exception of some media files (video, graphics, audio), all those Objects are special Motion files with the extension **.molo** (Motion Library Object) or **.mopr** (Motion Preview). Unlike regular media files which can be imported by dragging them from the Finder (besides using the File Browser), those Motion files can only be imported into a Project through the Library window.

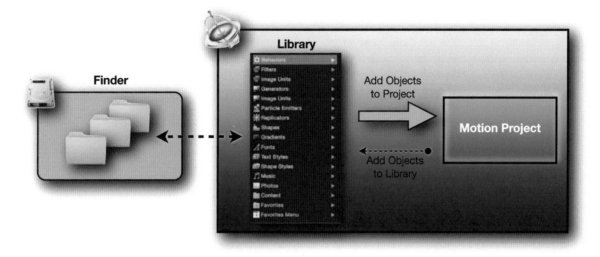

I included arrows in both directions in the diagram. That means that you can also save Objects back to the Library which get saved to the Finder and are then available in the Library as Custom Objects together with the Factory Objects.

Remember, whatever you do in the Library pane is general Motion content management on your local computer and is not related to your current Project. Any item you add, delete or edit in the Library is available to any future Project on your computer. But be careful, if you use any Objects from the Library in a Project and alter the Library file they are referring to later, then you might end up with a missing file in your Project that needs to be re-linked.

File Location

There are two main locations on your local drive for the Library Objects:

- Factory Objects: */Applications/Motion/Content/LibraryContent/*
- Custom Object: *"username"/Library/Application Support/Motion/Library/*

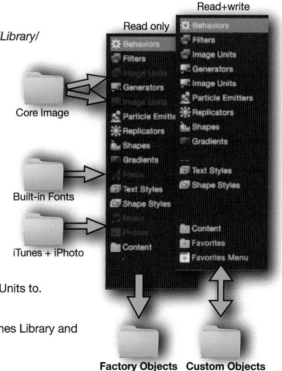

Each Category in the Library is represented by a folder with the same name in both of those locations. Selecting any category displays all the Objects it can find in both locations.

But not every Category (folder) is available in the Factory <u>and</u> Custom location. I try to demonstrate that in the diagram on the right. The left category list represents the available content in the Factory folder (read only) and the right list represents the Custom folder (read and write). I blocked out the categories which are not available as folders in that specific location.

There are five Categories that are exceptions:

- **Image Units**: These two folders (one for Filters and one for Generators) display the factory images from the Core Image system. Please note that the Custom location has those folders to copy Image Units to.
- **Fonts**: This folder displays all the available fonts on your computer.
- **Music, Photos**: These two folders display the content of your local iTunes Library and iPhoto Library.

Managing Library Objects

The Library provides some nice Object management and to better understand those mechanisms, think of three directions:

Drag Objects from the Library to the Project
Drag Object from the Library to the Library
Drag Object from the Project to the Library

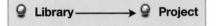

This is the standard procedure when you search for Objects in your Library that you want to add to your Project.

☑ Select a Category and Subcategory in the Sidebar.

☑ Enter a search phrase (optional).

☑ Drag the Object from the Stack to the Project (on the Project Pane, Timing Pane or Canvas).
Or click the "Apply" button in the Preview section of the Library window.

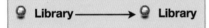

This has nothing to do directly with your Project. Here you just organize the Objects in the Library. By dragging a Factory Object from the Stack back to a Category, you create a Custom Object (a copy or an alias of that Object) in that Custom folder on your drive which is displayed immediately in the Library.

☑ Select a Category and Subcategory in the Sidebar.

☑ Drag an Object from the Stack back onto the Category in the Sidebar.

- To Same Category: The Library allows you to only move Objects into their own Category. And only a few Objects can be copied back into their own Category (Behavior, Filter, Filter Image, Generator, Image Generator, Font).

- To Favorites, Favorites Menu or Content: You can move any Object onto those Categories. In the Finder, Motion will create either a copy of that Object (Behavior, Filter, Filter Image, Generator, Image Generator, Font) or an alias (Emitter, Replicator, Shape, Gradient, Text Style, Shape Style).

Project ⟶ Library

You can use this step when you have an Object in your current Project that you want to add to the Library for later use. Maybe it is an Object that you really like or a standard Object that you often need in other Projects. The available Objects are Behavior, Filter, Generator, Emitter, Replicator, Shape and Text.

☑ Drag an Object from your Project (Project Pane, Timing Pane or Canvas) back onto the Library

- To Same Category: The Library allows you to only move Objects into their own Category

- To Favorites, Favorites Menu or Content: You can move any Object onto those Categories

Content Folder

This folder doesn't have a specific Category restriction. You can move different types of Objects there and organize them more freely especially with creation of custom folders and themes (see next page).

Favorites Folder

This is another folder without restriction to place and organize all your favorite Objects.

Favorites Menu Folder

Objects moved into this folder will be added to the Main Menu "Favorites". This is the fastest way to add an Object to your Project without opening the Library window, just select it from that Main Menu.

► **Custom Folder**

You can create custom folders on two different levels. The screenshots below show you how the Library corresponds with the actual files in the Finder (*"username"/Library/Application Support/Motion/*) ❶. It shows an example for the Generators folder (colored red in the Finder screenshot):

> 💡 **Add folders in a Subcategory list** (orange): Select the "All" folder in a subcategory list and click the "plus" button in the lower left corner of the Library.

> 💡 **Add folders in the Stack** (yellow): The Stack always displays the content of the selected folder in the Subcategory list. You will select one of those folders and click the "plus" button. The new folder will be created in the Stack.

You can rename the folders (select, hit return and type) and you can delete folders (select, Edit ➤ Delete). In the Stack, you can even drag Objects in and out of folder or into a folder in the Subcategory list.

You can also manage files and folders directly in the Finder as long as you follow the Category restrictions. The Library in Motion detects any changes in the Finder right away and displays them accordingly.

► **Favorites Menu**

The screenshots also display the relationship of the Objects placed in the "Favorite Menu" Category ❷. All those Objects in the Library ❸ will be displayed in the Favorites Main Menu ❹ which is a representation of the actual files in the "Favorites Menu" folder ❺ inside the Custom Library folder. In this example, you can see that some of the Objects are copies and some are aliases (with the arrow in the file icon). Of course, you can also create subfolders in the Stack and those folders will be displayed as submenus in the Favorites Main Menu.

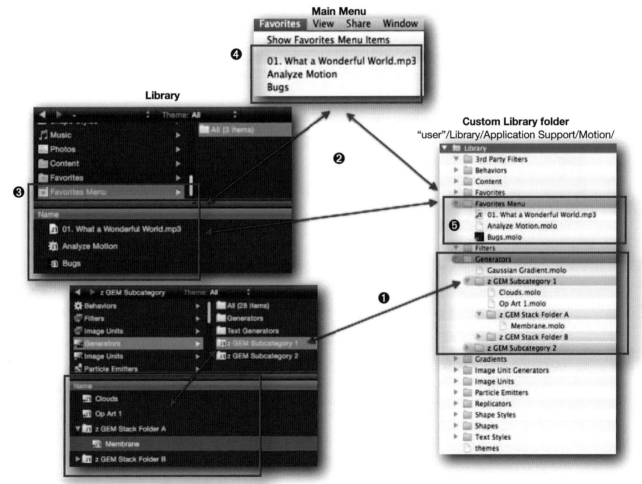

All the Custom Objects have a little "user" mini icon added to their standard icon for better identification:

► Shortcut Menu

Ctr+click on any Object in the Library will open its Shortcut Menu. Below are screenshots for the different Object types. You can Reveal the Finder location for any Object. Renaming and deleting is of course only available for Custom Objects, copies or aliases. A Custom Object that is a real copied file (and not an alias) has two extra menu items:

- 💡 **Edit Description**: The text you enter here will be displayed in the Preview section at the top of the Library window when you select that Object.

- 💡 **Theme**: This lets you assign a Library Theme to an Object.

► Library Themes

Above the Sidebar in the Library is a little popup menu named "Theme". The menu includes already 9 themes, but you can add your own themes with the "*New Theme ...*" command on that list.

When you **ctr+click** on a Custom Object in the Library to open its Shortcut Menu and select Theme, a submenu will display exactly those Themes. You can select one to assign that Theme to the Object. Later when you are in the Library and you select a specific Category and Subcategory, all the Objects in that Subcategory will be displayed in the Stack below. However, also selecting a Theme from the popup menu above the Sidebar will restrict the displayed Objects in the Stack to those which have that Theme assigned to it.

In the screenshot of the Custom Library folder on the previous page, you can see a file named "themes". This is an xml file that contains the names of your custom Themes.

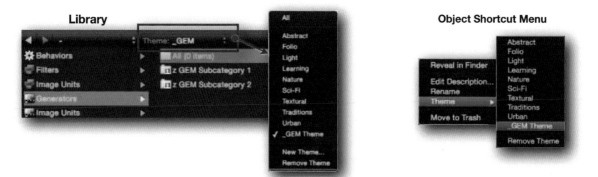

► Toolbar Access

The Motion Toolbar has three menu buttons on the right (Generators, Behaviors, Filters) that display the same content of those Categories in the Library for quick access without opening the Library window.

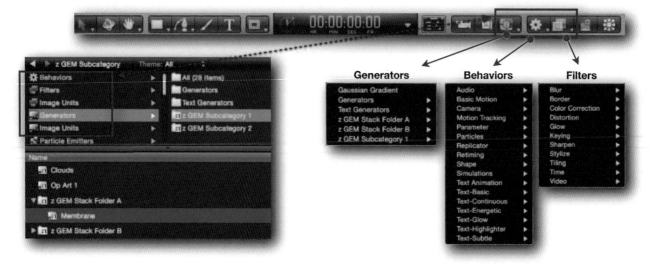

Create New Objects

To create new Objects from scratch, Motion provides buttons on the Toolbar that are grouped based on their functionality. Some buttons include a popup menu for more options:

💡 **Draw Objects**

These tools are similar to those in graphics applications. They let you draw various shapes (strokes are technically shapes too) or Masks (a special kind of shapes) or enter Text.

💡 **Add Objects**

Those three Objects can be added to your Project. The Camera and Light Object are Controller Objects for the 3D space where the Generators are computer-generated Image Objects.

💡 **Add Objects to existing Objects**

These tools require an existing Object in the Project. Behaviors and Filters are added to an existing Object like a plugin module where Particle Emitter and Replicator need an existing Object as their source.

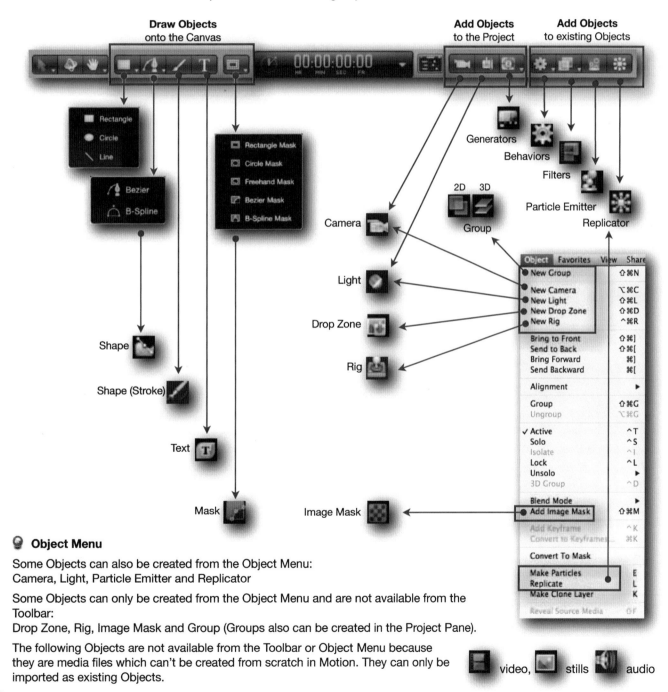

💡 **Object Menu**

Some Objects can also be created from the Object Menu:
Camera, Light, Particle Emitter and Replicator

Some Objects can only be created from the Object Menu and are not available from the Toolbar:
Drop Zone, Rig, Image Mask and Group (Groups also can be created in the Project Pane).

The following Objects are not available from the Toolbar or Object Menu because they are media files which can't be created from scratch in Motion. They can only be imported as existing Objects.

video,   stills   audio

5 - Project Pane

Overview

In order to discuss the three windows in the Project Pane, we have to be sure to understand the three underlying levels of your Motion interface:

▶ **Composition**

> This is your actual creation, the one you can view in the Canvas and that you export at the end when you are finished with it.

▶ **Motion Project**

> This includes your Composition, but also elements that you loaded into the Project but didn't use in your composition. This is what you save as a Motion Project file.

▶ **Motion Application**

> When you work in Motion, you actually work on a (single) Motion Project. However there are interface elements that are not part of your Project. For example, windows that are always the same, regardless of the current Project, i.e. File Browser, Library, Toolbar.

When we look at the Project Pane, it has three tabs to switch between three different views.

However, I think the logical order of the three tabs is wrong, because Layers and Audio belong to your Composition but Media belongs to your Project.

Project Pane

- 💡 **Layers List**

  > Contains all non-Audio Objects in your Composition

- 💡 **Audio List**

  > Contains all Audio-only Objects in your Composition

- 💡 **Media List**

  > Contains all media files in your Project

So the Layers list and the Audio list hold all the elements of your Composition. This is what is used in your Composition, the visual elements (Layers list) and the audio elements (Audio list).

The Media list on the other hand holds all the media files that you have loaded into your current Project. These are all the media files that are used in your Composition plus all the media files that are not used in your Composition but are still part of your Motion Project (in case you change your mind later or want to have alternate files available).

> You can toggle the whole Project Pane with the button in the lower left corner of the Canvas or use the Menu Command **Window ➤ Show/Hide Project Pane** or the Key Command **F5**.

The next page shows the mechanism detailing what ends up in what list when you drag or import Objects into your Motion Project:

	Layers	Audio	Media

Computer-graphics

Any computer-generated objects will only be listed in the Layers list (never in the Audio or Media list).

Media: Graphics

GraphicsFile.jpg

Dragging a graphics file to the Layers list (or through the import feature) will automatically place it into the Media list.

Dragging a graphics file into the Media list will not put it into the Layers list. It is not part of your Composition yet.

Media: Video (no audio)

VideoFile.mov

A video file without an audio track behaves like a graphics file regarding the import.

Media: Video (with audio)

VideoFile.mov

Dragging a video file, that includes audio, to the Layers list (or through the import feature) will place the video file into the Media list and the audio portion as an Audio Object into the Audio list.

Dragging that file to the Media List will not place it in the Layers list or Audio list.

Media: Audio

AudioFile.aif

Dragging an audio file to the Layers list (or with the import feature) will automatically place it to the Audio list and the Media list. It will not be placed in the Layers list, because that displays only the visual elements of your Composition.

Dragging that file to the Media List will not place it in the Layers or Audio list.

These Objects are part of your Composition

Importing or dragging a media file to the Layers or Audio list will put a reference of that file into the Media list and create an instance of that reference file in the Layers list (and/or Audio list) as an Object. You can drag a media file from the Media List onto the Canvas or Timing Pane to create more (independent) instances of that same file.

Media File (Finder) - **Reference** (Media List) - **Instance** (Layers list, Audio list)

Deleting Media File Objects

The deleting procedure depends on where you delete Objects from:

Preferences ➤ General

◉ Delete from the Layers or Audio List

The behavior depends on a checkbox in the Preferences: "Automatically manage unused media"

- **Unchecked**: deleting a media file object will keep its referred item in the Media list.
- **Checked**: deleting a media file object will also delete the item in the Media list if it is not used as another instance in your Composition. Motion will detect if a video file has a linked audio portion in the Audio list and prompts an alert window.

Objects that are not media files can be deleted from the Layers list any time because they are not linked to a media file.

One or more linked video objects will also be deleted. Are you sure you want to delete the audio?

You can delete just the audio by first unlinking it from the video.

Cancel | Delete

◉ Delete from the Media List

Deleting any media file from the Media List will also delete any existing instance of that file from the Layers or Audio List. An Alert window prompts a warning with a list of what the object names of those instances are.

One or more objects that use this media will also be deleted. Are you sure you want to delete the media used for these objects?

Beach video
Beach

Cancel | Delete

Layers List

The Layers List is the first view option in the Project Pane. The following commands will either switch to that view (if the Layers or Media view is visible) or toggle the whole Project Pane.

- Menu Command **Window ➤ Layers**
- Key Command **Cmd+4**
- Click on the Layers tab in the Project Pane (if the pane is not visible, click the disclosure button in the left lower corner of the Canvas)

The Layers List is a representation of your Composition.

▶ **What does it show**

It displays all the Objects in your Composition (except Audio Objects) and their relationship to each other, or to be precise: the hierarchy or stacking order of those Objects.

▶ **What does it NOT show**

You can't see any timing information about the Objects (when are they visible during the length of the Composition). This is what the Timing Pane is for. You also can't watch your Composition to see how it looks (the actual visual product of your Composition). This is what the Canvas is for.

Every item in the Layers List is an Object, a building block of your Composition.

Early on in this manual, I introduced all the available Objects in Motion and grouped them together based on their functionality or characteristics. Those characteristics now become important in the Layers list because there are rules about those Objects. Here there are the Objects again:

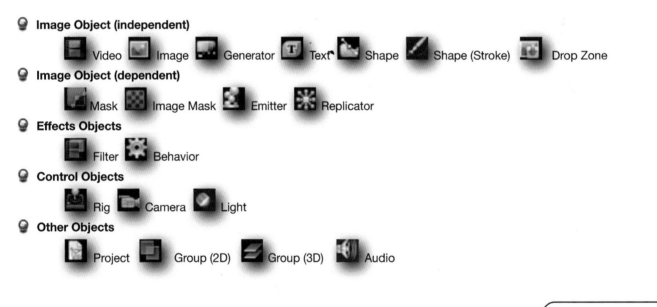

- **Image Object (independent)**
  Video   Image   Generator   Text   Shape   Shape (Stroke)   Drop Zone
- **Image Object (dependent)**
  Mask   Image Mask   Emitter   Replicator
- **Effects Objects**
  Filter   Behavior
- **Control Objects**
  Rig   Camera   Light
- **Other Objects**
  Project   Group (2D)   Group (3D)   Audio

All those Objects can show up in your Layers list (of course, with the exception of the Audio Object). But there is one new term that I haven't discussed so far. It is called a **Layer**.

> **Layer**

The Motion documentation defines a layer as *"a special class of object defined as any image-based element—a movie clip, a still image, a shape, text, a particle system, a replicator, and so on—that is visible in the Canvas"*

The term "Layer" is very common (also used in Photoshop) because it uses the physical model of using sheets of papers or photos and layer them in a specific way to create a graphical composition. The basic rules of that real-life model are used in the computer-graphics world. For example, putting one sheet of paper on top of another sheet of paper will cover the paper below unless the paper on top is transparent.

Motion uses the same terminology as the real-life model and computer-graphics application and uses it also in its motion-graphics application. However, a Layer is not another Object. A Layer is more of a label used for Image Objects. These are all the Objects that represent a visual Object like video clips, images, shapes and text. But also visual Objects that depend on other visual Objects like Masks, Emitter and Replicator. Effects and Controllers don't represent a visual Object, they process those Objects and therefore are not considered Layers.

Here is a screenshot of a simple Project next to the diagram of that Project and its available Objects.

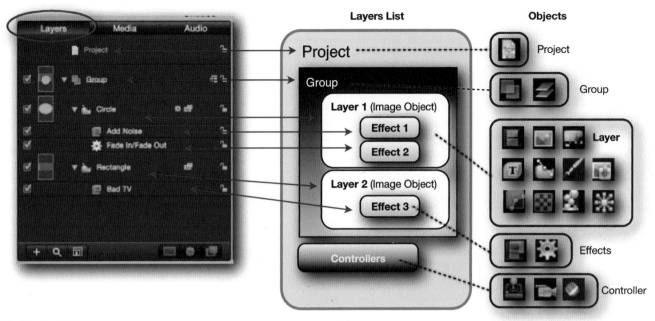

► **Basic Rules**

- Each Object in the list is placed on its own row which also provides buttons to control that Object.
- The first Object on top of the Layers list is the Project Object that represents the Composition in your Project. It can't be moved or deleted. Select it to view and edit the properties of your Project (cmd+J).
- Every Image Object that is imported or created in your Project becomes a Layer (there is no visual hint in the list as which row is a Layer and which one is not). It is just a definition: Any row with an Image Object is a Layer.
- A Layer must be enclosed in a Group Object.
- An Effects Object can be assigned to a Layer or a Group Object and is located underneath it with an indentation.
- Controllers can be placed anywhere, inside or outside a Group.

► **Group Rules**

- You can place as many Layers in a Group as you want.
- You can create different Groups for different Layers in order to group those Layers together for better organization or if you want to apply effects to a whole group.
- Groups can be placed inside another group (nested).
- New Image Objects will be placed into the first Group or the Group that is selected.
- Placing (or dragging) an Image Object onto the empty field at the bottom of the list will create a new Group at the top of the list and put the Layer in it.
- A Group can be switched between a 2D Group ▦ (default) and a 3D Group ◪ (i.e. click on the little Group icon next to the lock).

► **Organizing Rules**

- The list acts similarly to a folder/file structure in the Finder with disclosure triangles and indented views.
- The disclosure triangle lets you expand or collapse a row that contains other rows to better work in a long list.
- You can drag any row to anywhere in the list (opt+drag to copy). Guides and borders will indicate where the new placement will be when you release the mouse.
- You can (and should) rename each Object in a row to better identify it.
- Ctrl+click on any Object opens a Shortcut Menu with quick access to a variety of commands.

- ▶ **Layer Order**

  The list of all the Layers from top to bottom represents the stacking order of those Image Objects in your Composition. That means, the Image on top covers the next Image below it, which will then cover the next Image below that one, and so on. This is called the *Layer Order.* The exceptions to the stacking order are:

  - Images are placed next to each other (different X,Y coordinates)
  - Images have transparency or specific blend modes
  - Images are placed in a 3D space (they follow a Depth Order instead of the Layer Order)

Layers List Controls

The rows in the Layers list have a variety of small icons, controls and popup menus. They provide quick access to commands but also visual feedback. It is a good idea to get familiar with those subtle changes in appearance, especially when your list is growing longer and more complex.

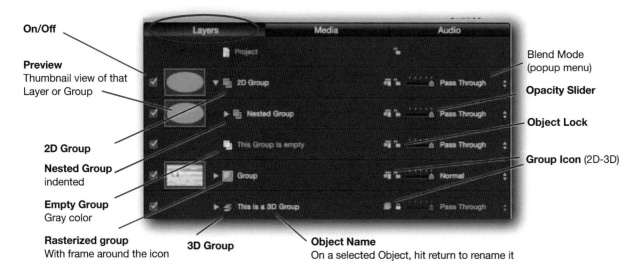

The three viewing elements Preview, Opacity and Blend Mode can be turned on or off from the Main Menu
View ➤ Layers Columns ➤

- ▶ **Selected / Isolate**

  The Selected /Isolate button has special functionality when working in 3D and is only visible for a selected Layer, Group or Camera if a Camera Object has been added to the Layers list. See the 3D chapter for details.

- ▶ **Preview**

The little Preview functions as a thumbnail which displays the content for that specific Layer. You can see how the stacking order of the different Layers will affect the overall image.

Please note that what you see is based on the current playhead position, even if the Layers list doesn't display any timing information. For example, if a Layer starts at 2s or has a fade in, then the Preview will be blank when the Playhead is parked at the beginning (0s).

The Preview however doesn't display changes in real time. It updates its view once the playhead stops or when you move the playhead to a different position.

Here is another screenshot with more controls:

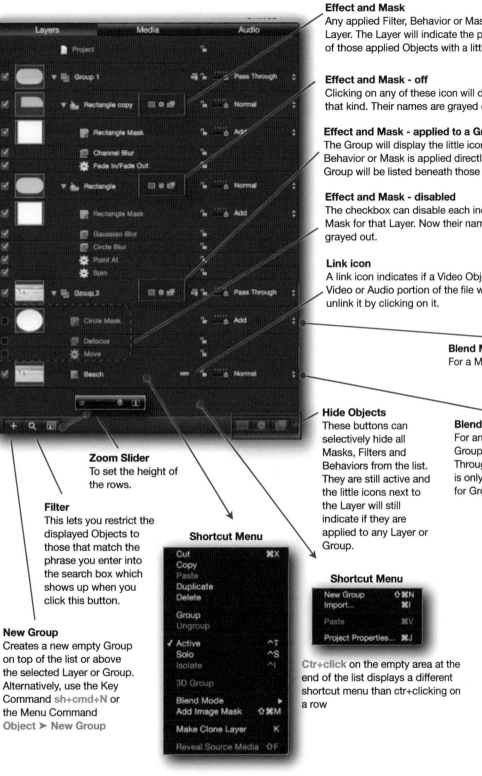

Effect and Mask
Any applied Filter, Behavior or Mask is placed indented below the Layer. The Layer will indicate the presence of one or more of any of those applied Objects with a little icon next to the Layer name.

Effect and Mask - off
Clicking on any of these icon will disable all applied Objects of that kind. Their names are grayed out if disabled.

Effect and Mask - applied to a Group
The Group will display the little icons in its row if a Filter, Behavior or Mask is applied directly to a Group. Any Layer in that Group will be listed beneath those Objects.

Effect and Mask - disabled
The checkbox can disable each individual Filter, Behavior or Mask for that Layer. Now their name and their Object icon is grayed out.

Link icon
A link icon indicates if a Video Object contains audio. Editing the Video or Audio portion of the file will affect both, unless you unlink it by clicking on it.

Blend Menu
For a Mask Layer

| ✓ Add |
| Subtract |
| Replace |
| Intersect |

Hide Objects
These buttons can selectively hide all Masks, Filters and Behaviors from the list. They are still active and the little icons next to the Layer will still indicate if they are applied to any Layer or Group.

Blend Menu
For any Layer or Group ("Pass Through" mode is only available for Groups)

| Pass Through |
| ✓ Normal |
| Subtract |
| Darken |
| Multiply |
| Color Burn |
| Linear Burn |
| Add |
| Lighten |
| Screen |
| Color Dodge |
| Linear Dodge |
| Overlay |
| Soft Light |
| Hard Light |
| Vivid Light |
| Linear Light |
| Pin Light |
| Hard Mix |
| Difference |
| Exclusion |
| Stencil Alpha |
| Stencil Luma |
| Silhouette Alpha |
| Silhouette Luma |
| Behind |
| Alpha Add |
| Light Wrap |

Zoom Slider
To set the height of the rows.

Filter
This lets you restrict the displayed Objects to those that match the phrase you enter into the search box which shows up when you click this button.

New Group
Creates a new empty Group on top of the list or above the selected Layer or Group. Alternatively, use the Key Command sh+cmd+N or the Menu Command Object ➤ New Group

Shortcut Menu

Cut	⌘X
Copy	
Paste	
Duplicate	
Delete	
Group	
Ungroup	
✓ Active	^T
Solo	^S
Isolate	^I
3D Group	
Blend Mode	▶
Add Image Mask	⇧⌘M
Make Clone Layer	K
Reveal Source Media	⇧F

Shortcut Menu

New Group	⇧⌘N
Import...	⌘I
Paste	⌘V
Project Properties...	⌘J

Ctr+click on the empty area at the end of the list displays a different shortcut menu than ctr+clicking on a row

⚡ Arranging Layers

The Object Menu contains a wide variety of commands that are known from Page Layout applications. Most of them are more useful when working in the Canvas where you can see the changes. However, some of the commands with their shortcuts can be used in the Layers list where you can see their effect right away.

- 💡 *Bring to Front* or *Back* moves the selected Object to the top or bottom of the Layers list.
- 💡 *Bring Forward/Send Backward* moves the selected Object up or down one position.

▶ Group / Ungroup

The Group command will put the selected Layer into its own Group and the Ungroup command resolved all the Layers in the selected Group (must be a nested Group) into the next higher level Group.

▶ Solo - Unsolo

This command will deactivate all Layers except the currently selected Layer(s) or Group(s). To un-solo it, use the command again or select another Layer and solo that one. You can also choose one of the selective Unsolo command from the submenu

▶ Clone Layers

You can clone specific Objects in the Layers list. This will create a special Clone Object that inherits the source Layers' attributes but can be treated individually (rearranged, placed, resized, etc). Any changes to the filter or masks in the source Layer will propagate through the Clone Layer. Other parameters can be edited independently.

Clone Layers can be identified by their special icon, a clone icon, added to the regular icon:

The following Objects can be cloned: video, graphics, shapes, text, particles, replicators and even groups.

To create a clone, select the object and choose any of those commands:

- 💡 Key Command K
- 💡 Menu Command Object ➤ Make Clone Layer
- 💡 Shortcut Menu Make Clone Layer

▶ Delete Objects

You can delete any selected Object from the Layers list with the standard commands: Hit the delete key, use the Delete or Cut command from the Edit Menu or the Shortcut Menu.

Special rules apply for deleting Objects referring to media files. See the paragraph "Deleting Media File Objects' at the beginning of this chapter.

▶ Copy Style

You can copy a style from one Object (Shapes and Text) to another Object of the same type. Just drag the Layer you want to copy over the Layer you want the style to copy to. By moving the mouse over the destination Layer without releasing the mouse button, an overlay pops up with the command "Copy Style to Shape".

Using the "Add Mask to Shape" command will move the source Layer to this destination Layer as a Mask.

Blend Modes

As we know by now, the Layers list displays the stacking order of your visual Objects (Layers and Groups). The hierarchy is from top to bottom where the top Layer covers the next Layer underneath and so on. The blend mode of each Layer (or Group) decides if it completely covers the next Layer or if the Layer on top lets the Layer below shimmer through. The different blend modes represent different mathematical calculations of how to "blend" the information of both Layers together (color, brightness, alpha channel, etc).

Here is an example with three Layers (A, B, C). In the diagram to the right, you can see a model where the three Layers are partially overlapping:

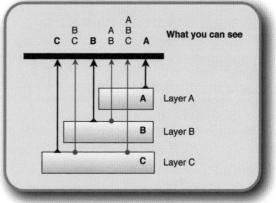

- The single letters represent an area that displays only that Layer.

- The double or triple letters represent the areas where the Layers are blended together. In the model, when the arrow of a bottom Layer has to go through a Layer above, then the blend mode of the Layer above decides how they will mix together, The product of that blend will be blended with the next Layer above based on its Blend Mode. Makes sense?

Here is a simple composite in the Layers list and how it looks in the Canvas:

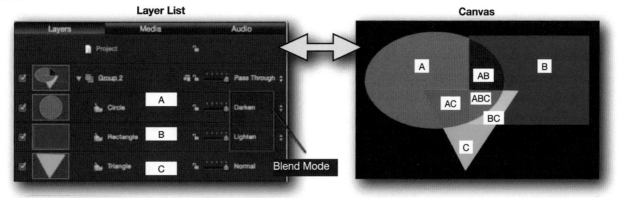

Pass Through

Here is an example with five Layers that demonstrate the "Pass Through" mode that is only available in a Group Object. If the Group is set to "Pass Through" then the Group functions just like an invisible container. All the Layers are acting as one big stack. If the Group is set to any other Blend Mode, then all the Layers below that Group can not blend with the individual Layers in the Group. They only can blend with the Group itself as the product of its Layers inside.

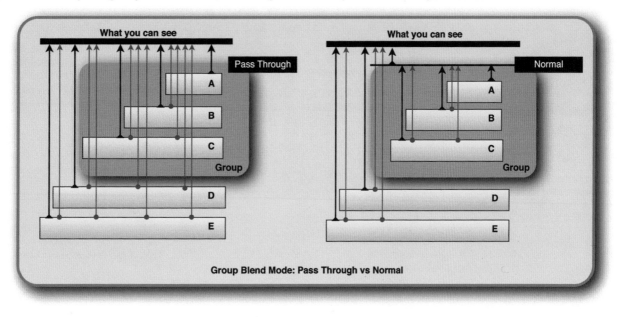

Group Blend Mode: Pass Through vs Normal

Audio List

The Audio List is the third view option in the Project Pane. The following commands will either switch to that view (if the Layers or Media view is visible) or toggle the whole Project Pane.

- **Window ➤ Audio**
- **Cmd+6**
- Click on the Audio tab in the Project Pane (if the pane is not visible, click the disclosure button in the left lower corner of the Canvas)

Motion is a motion-graphics application and as the word implies, the focus is on graphics, the visual elements. In that context, audio takes a little bit of a back seat. That's why you won't see any Audio Objects in the Layers List and of course not in the Canvas. But even if you don't "see" the audio Objects directly, you can make them visual, for example by controlling the visual elements in your Composition with audio. And that's how audio could become even more important than just adding audio objects to use as sound fx, music and dialog in your Project. Use Behavior Objects in conjunction with Audio Objects and you can create some cool audio-driven animation without opening the Keyframe editor once.

The interface elements of the Audio List are similar to the ones in FCPx. There is no conventional audio mixer. Every imported Audio Object (audio file or video file that contains audio tracks) is represented by a simple audio module and at the bottom there is the Master module.

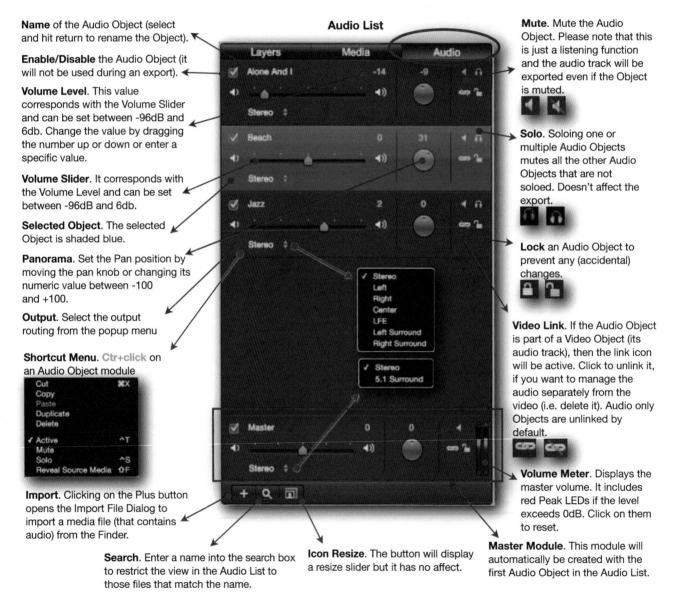

Name of the Audio Object (select and hit return to rename the Object).

Enable/Disable the Audio Object (it will not be used during an export).

Volume Level. This value corresponds with the Volume Slider and can be set between -96dB and 6db. Change the value by dragging the number up or down or enter a specific value.

Volume Slider. It corresponds with the Volume Level and can be set between -96dB and 6db.

Selected Object. The selected Object is shaded blue.

Panorama. Set the Pan position by moving the pan knob or changing its numeric value between -100 and +100.

Output. Select the output routing from the popup menu

Shortcut Menu. Ctr+click on an Audio Object module

Import. Clicking on the Plus button opens the Import File Dialog to import a media file (that contains audio) from the Finder.

Search. Enter a name into the search box to restrict the view in the Audio List to those files that match the name.

Icon Resize. The button will display a resize slider but it has no affect.

Mute. Mute the Audio Object. Please note that this is just a listening function and the audio track will be exported even if the Object is muted.

Solo. Soloing one or multiple Audio Objects mutes all the other Audio Objects that are not soloed. Doesn't affect the export.

Lock an Audio Object to prevent any (accidental) changes.

Video Link. If the Audio Object is part of a Video Object (its audio track), then the link icon will be active. Click to unlink it, if you want to manage the audio separately from the video (i.e. delete it). Audio only Objects are unlinked by default.

Volume Meter. Displays the master volume. It includes red Peak LEDs if the level exceeds 0dB. Click on them to reset.

Master Module. This module will automatically be created with the first Audio Object in the Audio List.

Audio Formats

Motion can read the following audio formats:

- AIFF, WAV, CAF, AAC, MP3, QuickTime
- Up to 32bit, up to 192kHz
- Mono, Stereo, Multichannel (Multichannel audio will be extracted to single tracks)
- DRM-protected files will not be imported

You can mix and match formats because Motion converts the audio file during the import to its internal format. When you export the Project, Motion converts the audio format to whatever format you choose in the Export settings.

Audio Adjustments

The controls in the Audio modules are also available in the HUD and the Inspector. Here is a comparison of those three available elements for an Audio Track and a Master Track.

The Properties tab in the Inspector provides additional timing parameters that reflect the trimming in the Audio Timeline.

Advanced Audio Adjustments

The Audio List window allows only simple audio adjustments. However, there are other areas in Motion that let you do more with your audio in your Project:

- 💡 **Audio List**: Make basic audio adjustments for level and pan.
- 💡 **Audio Timeline**: Trim your Audio Object in the Timing Pane like video clips to determine the timing position in the Project and automate their parameters in the Keyframe Editor (covered in the Timing Pane Chapter).
- 💡 **Keyframe Editor**: Automate the parameter of the Audio Object.
- 💡 **Behaviors**: Like with any other Object, you can use Behaviors with Audio Object.
  - Audio Behavior: Apply a Behavior to the Audio Object that controls it.
  - Audio Parameter Behavior: Use the Audio Object as a source for a Behavior that controls another Object.

Here is a closer look at those two concepts:

💡 Audio Behavior

You assign an Audio Behavior to an Audio Object that functions like an effects plugin. This is the same principle as with any other Image Object to which you assign a Behaviors Object to it. You can edit the Parameter in the Behavior tab of the Inspector or in the HUD

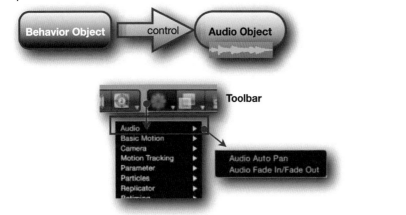

💡 Audio Parameter Behavior

Here you have an Image Object. You assign also a Behavior to it, however, the type of Behavior is an "Audio Parameter Behavior." This means you can select an existing Audio Object from the Audio list as the Source Audio that controls any of the available Parameters of that Image Object. The Behavior tab of the Inspector for the Image Object lets you configure it (i.e. increase the size of an object through the rhythm of a pumping bass drum in a song).

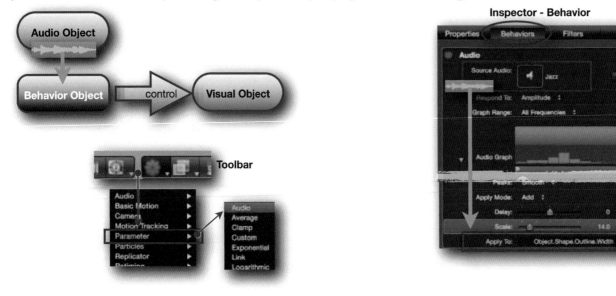

Media List

The Media List is the second view option in the Project Pane. The following commands will either switch to that view (if the Layers or Audio view is visible) or toggle the whole Project Pane.

- Window ➤ Media
- Cmd+5
- Click on the Media tab in the Project Pane (if the pane is not visible, click the disclosure button in the lower left corner of the Canvas)

This is what you see in the list:

- Only media files (videos, images, audio), no computer-generated files.
- All media files that have been imported into your Project regardless if they are used in your actual Layers List or not.
- The media files in the list are only references to the actual file on your drive. Those files are never altered by any of your settings in your Motion Project (Motion's File Browser and Library window however affect files on your drive).

The interface is pretty simple as it follows standard list view conventions.

Media List

Media: Shortcut Menu

List Header:
- Click to sort by that column
- Sort ascending/descending
- Rearrange header by dragging
- Ctr+click to open shortcut menu

Header: Shortcut Menu

List: Shortcut Menu

Opens the "Import Files" dialog   Search the list   Zoom Slider: list rows

Media List

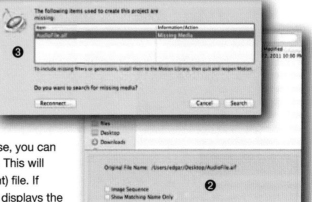

If the Project contains a reference to a media file that it cannot find anymore (renamed, moved or deleted in the Finder), then the Preview column will display a question mark icon ❶. In that case, you can use the "Reconnect Media ..." command from the Shortcut Menu. This will open a dialog window ❷ to search for the original (or a replacement) file. If Motion cannot locate a file during launch, then a Dialog window ❸ displays the missing files that you can search for or reconnect.

Media Files Inspector

Please be clear about the difference between the Layers and Audio list versus the Media list regarding media files: Every media file that you import into your Project is listed in the Media list (used or unused). Only the used media files that you use in your Composition are in the Layers list (visual media files) and the Audio list (audio media files).

If you select a media file in the Layers list or Audio list and select the Inspector, then the fourth tab (the *Object Tab)* will be labeled "Image" or "Audio Track". Those tabs include the attributes of that instance. If you select the same file in the Media list, then the fourth tab of the Inspector window displays "Media" for editing the attributes of the media reference file.

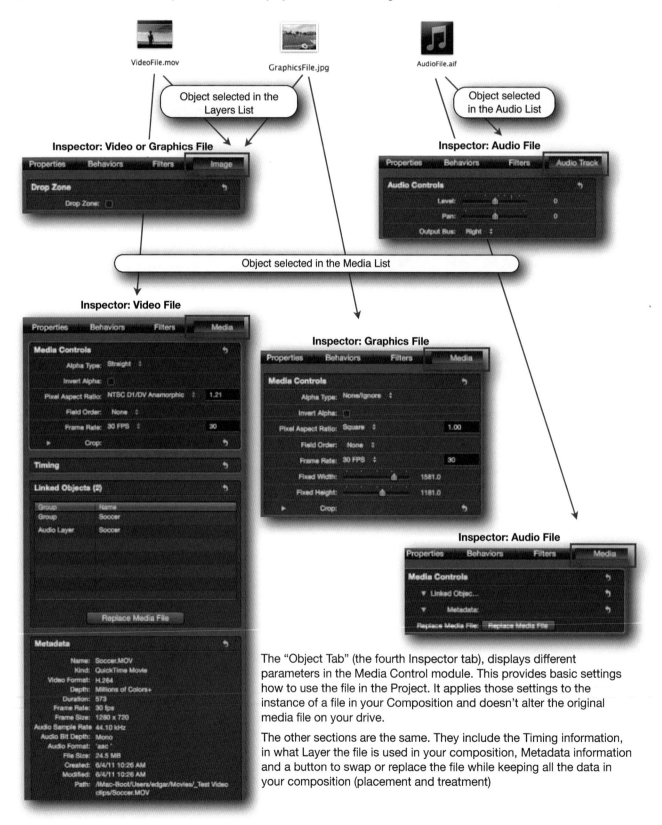

The "Object Tab" (the fourth Inspector tab), displays different parameters in the Media Control module. This provides basic settings how to use the file in the Project. It applies those settings to the instance of a file in your Composition and doesn't alter the original media file on your drive.

The other sections are the same. They include the Timing information, in what Layer the file is used in your composition, Metadata information and a button to swap or replace the file while keeping all the data in your composition (placement and treatment)

6 - Timing Pane

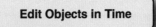

The Timing Pane has three individual timeline windows for different purposes. They let you view and edit the Objects in your composition with a focus on their change in time. Unlike the other window panes in Motion where you can view only one selection at a time, here you can show/hide any of the three views separately. The three window views are:

💡 **Video Timeline**

This window provides a typical track-based timeline like in FCP7, displaying the Objects in your Composition as clips. The difference is that this timeline displays only visual objects, no audio objects. It provides a view how all the non-audio Objects are laid out over time.

Toggle the window with **cmd+7** or Menu Command **Window ➤ Video Timeline** or click the Video button in the right lower corner:

💡 **Audio Timeline**

This timeline works the same way. However, it displays only the Audio Objects of your Composition. It provides a view of how all the audio-only Objects are laid out over time.

Toggle the window with **cmd+9** or Menu Command **Window ➤ Audio Timeline** or click the Audio button in the right lower corner:

💡 **Keyframe Timeline**

Although the Video Timeline and the Audio Timeline can display Keyframes too, this Timeline provides extended tools to view and edit Keyframes to visualize the animation curves for animated parameters.

Toggle the window with **cmd+8** or Menu Command **Window ➤ Keyframe Editor** or click the Keyframe button in the right lower corner:

One command toggles the whole Timing Pane regardless what combination of the Timeline is visible at the moment. If all the individual Timelines where hidden, then this command will open only the Video Timeline as a default view:

Menu Command **Window ➤ Show/Hide Timing Pane** or Key Command **F6**

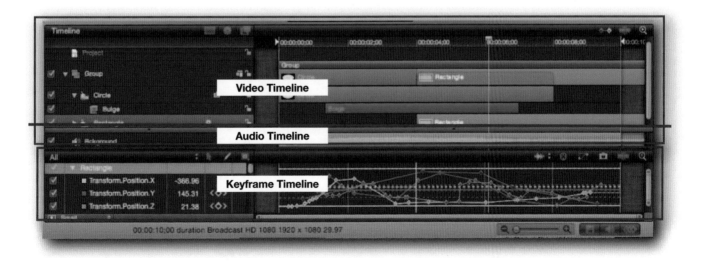

The official Motion documentation uses a different terminology for the three windows: Timeline - Audio Timeline - Keyframe Editor. However, I prefer the terms "Video Timeline", "Audio Timeline" and "Keyframe Timeline", because they indicate better that they all belong to the Timing Pane (I use the term "Video" as in "visual elements", all the non-audio objects).

Let's have a closer look at the interface before going into the details about the individual controls and editing tools. Here is a screenshot where all three views are visible. Pay attention to the difference of the three views regarding the interface elements.

- All three views share the same Timeline Ruler ❶.

- The Playhead ❷ also spans across all the available Timeline views.

- The Keyframe Timeline has its own Header ❸. The upper edge of that header functions as the divider line where you drag to resize the height of the window.

- The Video and Audio Timeline share the same header ❹. When both views are visible, it looks like the Audio Timeline is just an add-on Timeline with a divider line to resize the windows.

- All three views are divided into two sections, the List ❻ to the left and the Track Area ❺ to the right. You can drag the divider line between to resize the sections.

- At the lower right corner (part of the always visible Motion frame) ❼ are the three view buttons and a zoom slider that zooms the Timeline horizontally. You can also drag the edges of the scroll bar or use two finger pinch on a Trackpad.

Timing Pane

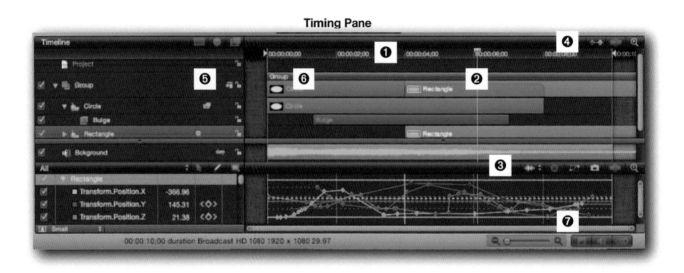

When you show and hide any of the three windows, they resize their height automatically to fit into the available size of the Timing Pane window. You can drag the divider line between the Toolbar and Timing Pane to resize the overall height of the Timing Pane (affecting the size of the Canvas) and also drag the line between the individual Timeline to resize their height in relation to each other. If you hide the last Timeline, then the whole Timing Pane disappears (expanding the Canvas).

You can move the whole Timing pane to a second connected Monitor with the following Menu Command:

Window ➤ Show Timing Pane on Second Display

Timeline Ruler

The displayed units in the Timeline Ruler can be switched between Frames and SMPTE timecode in the Time Display popup menu. Here you set also the display mode of the Time Display to show the Current Time (of the current Playhead position).

Adding Objects

The position of the Playhead (indicated by the Time Display) is important because it determines where an Object is placed on the Timeline when added to your Project. The Preferences window provides a setting that determines if that is the default behavior. You can set it to "*Start of project*" or "*Current frame*" which means the Object will be placed at the position of the Playhead.

Video and Audio Timeline

The Video Timeline and Audio Timeline have two sections. On the left, the Layers List and on the right, the Track Area. Each row in the Layers List (representing an Object) continues through the vertical divider into the Track Area where the same Object is displayed as a single Clip, laid out on a track over time. I prefer the term "clip" instead of object, item, region or even "timebar" which is used in Apple's documentation. These "timebars" behave more like clips on video tracks when it comes to editing and trimming.

Track Height

The little popup menu in the lower left corner of the Timeline window lets you resize the rows. You can also drag the divider line between the rows.

Video / Audio Timeline

The main purpose for those timeline windows is to view and edit your Objects in the timing context of your Project. You can see where each object starts and ends, and you can see that in relation to the placement of all the other objects in your Project. Although it looks more like old fashioned FCP7 video tracks, it is functioning more like viewing and editing your video clips on a FCPx timeline (without the primary storyline). Even the color code is similar with green for audio objects and blue for video objects.

Timeline Layers List

This is the same list as the Layers List in the Project Pane. It also functions the same and the only exception is that there are a few elements which are not displayed here in the list, like Preview, Opacity and Blend Mode. This list even has an advantage over the Project Pane. Here in the Timing Pane, you can view the Layers List and the Audio List at the same time.

You also have the same show/hide buttons in the header for Masks, Behaviors and Filters.

Pay attention to the Objects in the list in regards to their placement on the Timeline Track. In the example above, the Playhead is parked at a position before the beginning of the Rectangle Object and its assigned Behavior. At this position those two Objects are inactive (not visible). That's why they are grayed out in the Layers list (and also in the Project Pane's Layers list)

Adding Objects

All the rules for adding Objects to the Layers List in the Project Pane also apply to the Layers list here in the Timing Pane. You can drag Objects directly onto the Layers list.

However, you might want to drag the Objects directly onto the Track Area. This way, you're not only determining where you place the Object in the stacking order, but also where to place it in time.

Timeline Track Area

First let's look at the interface elements.

In the upper right corner of the Timeline are three buttons:

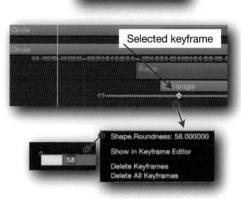

Keyframes   Snapping   Zoom To Fit

💡 **Keyframes**

When activated, each track will extend its height a little to display a keyframe lane. This is a quick way to see which Object has keyframes programmed. You won't see the actual curve, only the presence of the keyframes. However, you have some limited edit capabilities without the need of opening the Keyframe Timeline.

The red Keyframes turn white when you select them. **Ctr+Click** on a keyframe opens a Shortcut Menu with the following commands:

- *The Value of the keyframe*. Selecting it will open another window that lets you enter a new value.

- *Show in Keyframe Editor*. This opens the Keyframe Timeline for more detailed editing of that keyframe.

- *Delete Keyframes* (only the selected ones) or *Delete All Keyframes* for that parameter.

💡 **Snapping**

When you drag an Object, it will snap to the edges of the nearest Object. **Sh+drag** will inverse snap mode (if snap is on, then it will disable it and if it is off, then it will enable it as long as you hold the shift key while you're dragging an object).

Please note that there are two different snap modes. Menu Command **View ➤ Snap** or Key Command **N** toggle the other snap mode for Objects in the Canvas.

💡 **Zoom To Fit Project**

A click on the magnifier button zooms the Timeline vertically to fit the Project.

Clip Display

The Preferences window lets you configure how the Clips ("Timebar") will be displayed in the Track area.

Other Elements

Here are other elements in the timeline

Navigation

💡 Play Range

This is a playback setting that limits the Project to be played only between the In and Out Markers. Playback will stop at the out marker (if Loop playback is off) and Loop playback will be restricted to that range, although you can start before the *Mark In* by placing the Playhead there.

The Mark Menu provides commands to set the Mark Play Range In and Mark Play Range Out point to the current Playhead position (you can use the Mark In and Mark Out command if no Object is selected). The area outside the Play Range gets a darker shade.

Reset Play Range sets the In and Out to the beginning and end of the Project.

💡 In and Out Points

The Mark In and Out command trims the start or end of the selected Clip(s) to the playhead position.

The Move Selected In Point or Move Selected Out Point command moves the selected Clip(s) so its beginning or end point aligns with the playhead.

💡 Navigation

The third section of the Mark Menu and the Go to submenu list all the navigation commands. Alternatively, you can use their Key Commands or the navigation buttons on the Canvas.

💡 RAM Preview

This renders the Range, Selection or the whole Project into RAM to allow proper playback of complex Compositions that might be too much for your CPU to handle in real time. Of course, the usability depends on your available RAM.

💡 Markers

The Markers submenu contains all the related commands. Create a marker on any selected Object on a track, even on the Timeline itself if nothing else is selected. The Edit Marker... command opens a separate window that lets you enter a Name, Comment, Color, Start and even a Duration to create a Marker range.

Create a Marker on the selected Object(s) from the Main Menu Mark ➤ Add Marker or the Key Command M (can be created during playback). This will create a Project Marker if no Object is selected (or sh+click on the Timeline)

Ctr+click on a Marker or the Timeline will display the Shortcut Menu for more commands

Marker Shortcut Menu

The Markers can be used as a visual reference, to align Objects with the snap mode or to add notes to a sections of your Project. Those Markers can also be used for Final Cut Templates.

Audio Scrubbing

Opt+drag the Playhead will scrub the audio. The audio will loop the 5 frames around the position when you stop moving the mouse in that mode without releasing the mouse.

Editing Clips

▶ **Add Objects**

Of course, any Object dragged onto the Timeline will immediately be displayed in the Layers list of the Timeline and Project pane and also in the Canvas. The advantage of adding Objects onto the Timeline is that you control both, the placement in the hierarchy (vertical) and the placement in time (horizontal).

If you drag an Object and wait a moment, an overlay menu will be displayed with the following choices. (Composite will be the default if you don't wait for the menu and release the mouse right away). What kind of choices are available depends on what Object you are adding and what Object you are adding it to:

Various Choices for Adding Objects to the Timeline

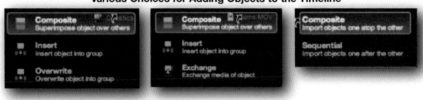

○ **Composite**: The new Object will be placed on a new track at the timeline position of your mouse.

○ **Insert**: The new Object will be placed on a new track at the timeline position of your mouse. Any existing Clip after that drop point will be moved to the right by the length of the new clip. Any Clip that spans across the insert point will be split and the second part of that split Clip will be placed on a separate Track (as a new Layer).

○ **Overwrite**: The new Object will be placed on a new track at the timeline position of your mouse, replacing the existing Clip. If the new Clip is shorter than the existing one, then the existing Clip will be split and put on a separate track.

○ **Exchange**: The new Object will be placed on a new track at the timeline position of your mouse. However, there are two extra rules. First, the new Clip replaces the existing one from the drop point but only for the length of the existing clip. Second, the new clip inherits all the effects of the clip it replaces.

○ **Sequential**: If you drag multiple Objects at the same time, then all the new Objects will be placed on new tracks on the timeline. This time, the first one starts at the position of your mouse on top of the hierarchy, the second clip starts at the end of the first one and continues in sequential order (selecting Composite when dragging in multiple Objects will place them all at the same Timeline position).

Layer Order

The horizontal position of your drop decides where the new clip is positioned in time (watch out for the tooltips with the timing info). However, it is also important where you position your mouse vertically. Moving it over a Group will place the new clip as the top Layer in that group. Positioning it between two tracks will place it between those two Layers. Look out for the visual guides.

▶ **Move Clips**

○ **Drag**

Drag the Clip(s) to move them to a new position on the track (horizontally only). A yellow tooltip will appear during the drag, displaying the new In and Out and the "delta" which indicates how far you moved the clip away from its original position.

Move Clip

○ **Enter a numeric value:**

- **Specific frame**: Select the Clip, type a frame value (a value box appears), hit enter and the clips moves to that frame address.

Enter frame number

- **Specific offset**: Select the Clip, type a Timecode value starting with a plus or minus sign (a value box appears in the Timeline while you are typing), hit enter and the Clip moves by that amount.

Enter timecode offset

- **Trim Clips**
  - **Drag**

    Trim Clip

    Drag the edge of the beginning or ending of a clip to shorten or lengthen that section. A tooltip window displays the In, Out and amount of the offset. For video or audio objects, a dimmed area displays during dragging how much footage is available on that side of the clip. Those objects cannot be extended beyond the end of their clip unless you activated "Loop" in the objects properties. Using the Retiming tool also extends the original length of a media file.

  - **Command**

    You can use also Key Commands or Menu Commands from the Mark menu to trim the In or Out of the selected clip(s) to the playhead position (even during playback).

- **Slip Clips (video only)**

  Slip Clip

  Similar to conventional video editing, this procedure lets you move the underlying content of the source media file without changing the position and length of the clip.

- **Other Editing Tools**

  - **Copy - Paste**

    You can copy and paste Clips with the standard commands. The clips will be pasted at the playhead position at the top of the selected Group or its original Group (if none is selected). If the Clip came from a different Project, then a new Group will be created for it.

    Choosing the Menu Command Edit ➤ Paste Special will open a window with three selections to Insert, Overwrite or Exchange, similar to the add Objects behavior.

  - **Delete**

    Deletes the Clip(s) (and its timeline track) and leaves everything else in place. Use the Key Command delete or the Menu Command Edit ➤ Delete.

  - **Ripple Delete**

    Deletes the Clip(s) and its timeline track and moves everything else to the left to fill the gap. Use the Menu Command Edit ➤ Ripple Delete.

  - **Insert Time**

    Opt+cmd+drag a range in the timeline and use the Menu Command Edit ➤ Insert Time to split all the Clips into two tracks at the left edge of that range and move everything to the right by the amount of the range length.

  - **Loop**

    Sh+opt+drag the end of a clip to loop it. The tooltip displays the percentage and new duration of the clip. Detailed settings are in the Inspector's Timing Properties under "End Condition".

    Loop Clip

  - **Splitting Objects**

    Use the Menu Command Edit ➤ Split to split a selected Clip at the playhead position into two Clips, putting the second portion on a new track. The new Clip (Layer) inherits all the applied effects and both can be edited now independently.

    Retime Clip

  - **Retime**

    Opt+drag the end of a clip to change the original playback speed of a video clip. The tooltip displays the percentage and new duration of the clip.

💡 Group Editing

The Clip that represents a Group has two sections on its track. The upper section represents the Group itself as one long Clip. The lower sections of the track display all the included Clips. If Clips overlay, then the clips will merge and show individual parts if possible, depending on how the clips overlap.

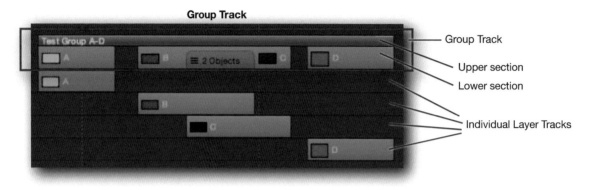

Any kind of clip editing that involves dragging the actual Clip can be performed on the Clip itself or on the Group Clip (lower section). You could manipulate the enclosed Clips in the lower section of the Group track if the Group Layer is collapsed and you can't see the individual hidden tracks.

The boundaries of the Group Clip are defined by the left edge of the first clip and the right edge of the last clip in the Group. The Group Clip and the enclosed Layer Clips are connected. Moving the Group Clip moves all the enclosed Clips as one unit. Trimming any of those outer edges of the Group Clip trims the edges of the Clip that defines that border. However, you can disconnect this tie by trimming the edges independently when you **cmd+drag** those edges. To reestablish that tie, align the boundaries of the Group Clip to the two Layer Clips on both ends.

💡 Region Editing

This is a special kind of editing where you can define an editing range by dragging a Region. Any editing command will apply only to that selected range. These are the steps:

- ☑ **Opt+cmd+drag** in the timeline to select a Region as a highlighted band
- ☑ Drag the Region to move it (optional)
- ☑ **Cmd+click** on a track to deselect that Clip from the Region (optional)
- ☑ Select a command:

  Delete or Ripple Delete

  Copy the Range and Paste the whole content of the Region to the playhead position

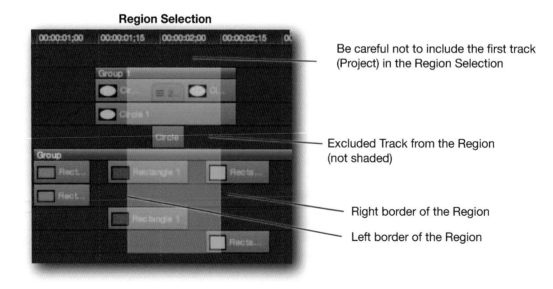

Be careful not to include the first track (Project) in the Region Selection

Excluded Track from the Region (not shaded)

Right border of the Region

Left border of the Region

Keyframe Timeline

The third window in the Timing Pane is the Keyframe Timeline which lets you animate (automate) virtually any parameter of an Object over time. Each parameter can be displayed as an animation curve in a graph, where the x-axis is the time and the y-axis is the value of that parameter. You can create those animation curves by creating single x/y-coordinates (called keyframes). Motion connects those keyframes (interpolate) to create the final animation line. I explain the whole concept of Keyframes and the mathematical background in more detail in my manual "Final Cut Pro X - The Details".

Here is the basic principle:

The example shows the graph in the Keyframe Timeline displaying the Opacity value of an Object.

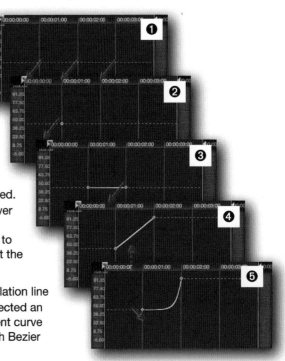

❶ This is the default view where no Keyframe has been set for the Opacity. The graph displays only one dotted line which represents the current value for the Opacity. In this example, it is 50%, constant throughout the Project. Changing the Opacity in the Inspector will move the line up or down.

❷ Here I created a Keyframe at 1s with the value of 50%. Technically, nothing has changed. The Opacity stays constant throughout the Project. You can also change the value of the Opacity now directly in the graph by dragging the Keyframe up and down.

❸ Here I created a second Keyframe at 2s with the same value of 50%. Again, nothing changes in regards to the Opacity. It stays the same. However, the line between the two Keyframes is solid, it is called an "animation line" or "interpolation line". The line before the first Keyframe and after the last Keyframe is still dotted.

❹ Now I dragged the second Keyframe up to 100%. Two things happened. The interpolation line still connects the two frames. The difference however is that it creates (interpolates) invisible Keyframes between the two keyframes to simulate a gradual increase of the Opacity value from 50% to 100% when the Project plays between 1s and 2s. The second fact is that the dotted line after the last Keyframe stays at that value (100%) to the end.

❺ Here the Keyframes are unchanged. The difference is how the interpolation line is drawn, the shape of the line (curved). Instead of a linear increase, I selected an exponential curve. From a Shortcut Menu, you can choose from 6 different curve types. One of them is a Bezier curve that you can shape even further with Bezier control point handles.

Please note that the behavior of the Inspector changes after the first Keyframe has been set for a parameter. It is called the "Initial Keyframe Method". See below for more details.

So every animation curve is defined by two elements: Keyframes and Interpolation Lines.

💡 **Keyframes**

This is a specific value at a specific time in your project. Please keep in mind that, once it is created, you can change that Keyframe directly in a graph or you can change the control in the Inspector, or the Canvas which is a representation of the Keyframe. Another thing to be aware of is that some controls affect one Keyframe (i.e. Opacity) while other controls are a combination of two or more Keyframes, i.e. the Scale changes the X, Y and Z Keyframe (Compound Parameter).

💡 **Interpolation Lines**

There are two types of lines. Both have their own Shortcut Menu to choose a specific type of curve

- Between two Keyframes
- Before/After the first and last Keyframe: The first and last Keyframe don't have to be at the first and last frame of your Project. If they are not, then a constant (dotted) line extends to the first and from last Keyframe. However, you can choose a different curve from the popup menu.

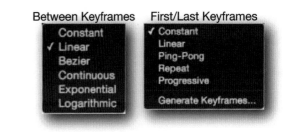

Between Keyframes	First/Last Keyframes
Constant	✓ Constant
✓ Linear	Linear
Bezier	Ping-Pong
Continuous	Repeat
Exponential	Progressive
Logarithmic	Generate Keyframes...

Interface Elements

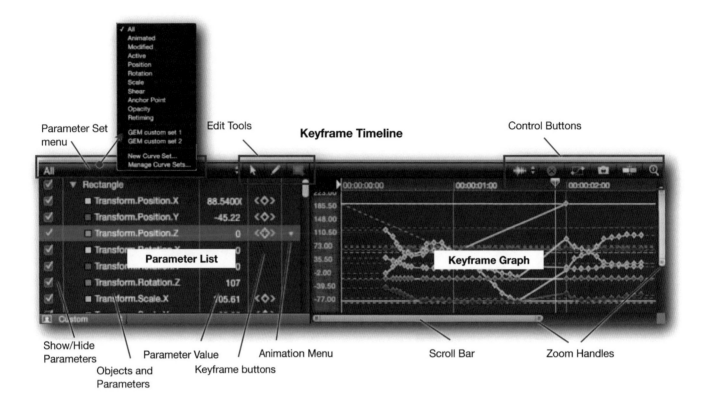

Parameter Set menu

Edit Tools

Keyframe Timeline

Control Buttons

Parameter List

Keyframe Graph

Show/Hide Parameters

Parameter Value

Animation Menu

Scroll Bar

Zoom Handles

Objects and Parameters

Keyframe buttons

The two main sections in the Keyframe Timeline are the Parameter List and the Keyframe Graph. However, think about the whole interface as a three step process:

☑ Object

First, select one (or multiple) Object in any of the other windows (Project Layers List, Timeline Layers List, Canvas) that you want to view in the Keyframe Timeline.

☑ Parameter

The Parameter List on the left displays the parameters of that selected Object(s). The Parameter Set menu acts like a filter. It lets you display specific parameters or groups of parameters.

☑ Graph

The Keyframe Graph on the right displays the curves for all the parameters in the Parameters List. Please note that all the parameters share one timeline track with color coding for better identification of the individual curves.

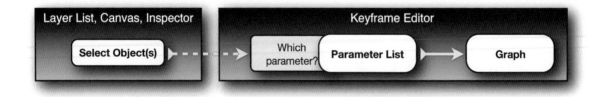

Parameter List

The Graph only displays the Keyframes for parameters that are on the Parameters List. The two criteria that determine what is displayed in the Parameters List are the selected Object (in a different window) and the selected Parameter Set that filters out specific parameters of all the available parameters for an Object.

► **Parameter Sets (Curve Sets)**

This is the popup menu in the left upper corner of the Keyframe Timeline. Instead of the official name "Curve Sets", I prefer "Parameter Sets" because you are selecting Parameters and not Curves. The different sets are like viewing presets that decide which parameter(s) of the currently selected Object(s) will be displayed in the list. Of course, an Object can be selected in any of the windows (Project Pane, Canvas, Timeline). You can also create your own parameter sets.

- *All*: Displays all the parameters of all selected Object(s).
- *Animated*: Displays only the parameters of the selected Object(s) that already have Keyframes.
- *Modified*: Displays only the parameters of the selected Object(s) who's default value has changed (manually or through Keyframes).
- *Active*: Displays only the parameter that you are currently modifying (clicking on it) in the Inspector, HUD or Canvas.
- "*Various parameters*": These are sets of often used parameters.
- "*Custom sets*": Displays your sets that you created with the 'New Curve Set' command.
- *New Curve Set...*: Opens a window to enter a name for your new Set. The new custom set will include all the currently visible parameters. You can now remove any Parameter from the list (select, delete) or drag another parameter directly from the Inspector onto the list. It is that simple. Custom Curve Sets are stored with your Project not with the Motion application.
- *Manage Curve Sets...*: Opens a window that lets you add or remove custom sets.

► **Parameter List**

The list can display two types of line items. The selected Object and the individual Parameters for that Object. The displayed Object (with a disclosure triangle) is the one that is selected in another window (Video Timeline, Layers List, Canvas). If you've selected multiple Objects, then all those Objects with their parameters are displayed in this list. Don't forget that a Group is also an Object with its own parameters that you can animate. Here are the columns in the list:

- **On/off**: Show/hide the curve for that parameter in the graph.
- **Names**: The name of the Object or Parameter.
- **Value**: The value for the parameter at the current playhead position.
- **Keyframe Buttons**: The visibility of the buttons is context sensitive. This is for adding and deleting individual Keyframes. It also lets you jump to the next and previous Keyframe. The functionality of those buttons is the same as in FCPx which I cover in depth in my manual "FCPx - The Details".
- **Animation menu**

    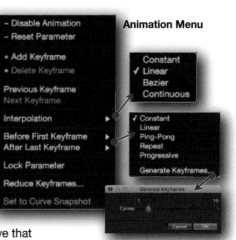

    - *Enable/Disable Animation*: This bypasses the animation curve and sets it to the value of the last Keyframe in the graph. The Keyframe Button column displays a hyphen to indicate this mode.
    - *Reset Parameter*: Deletes all Keyframes for this parameter and restores its default value.
    - *Add/Delete Keyframe*: At the current playhead position.
    - *Previous Keyframe, Next Keyframe*: Moves the playhead to the next or previous Keyframe.
    - *Interpolation* menu: Select an interpolation curve from the menu. This applies to ALL interpolation lines for that parameter. For individual segments use the Shortcut Menu by ctr+clicking on the curve or keyframe in the graph.
    - *Before First Keyframe, After Last Keyframe*: Select an extrapolation curve that determines the look of the curve before the first frame and after the last frame.

- *Lock Parameter*: This is very useful if you display multiple parameters in the graph and want to avoid overwriting the wrong parameter by accident. The locked Keyframes are grey.

- *Reduce Keyframes...*: A window will be displayed that provides a slider (Error Tolerance) to thin out Keyframes and a second slider (Smoothing) to smooth out the curve. These controls come in handy if you've recorded movements online or used the Sketch tool offline.

- *Set Curve Snapshot*: This is a special "undo" feature. Before you experiment with some animation, take a snapshot of the current curve with the snapshot tool and do all the changes. If the new changes don't work out, select the "Set Curve Snapshot" which replaces the curve with the snapshot, including all its Keyframes.

Snapshot button

Tools

The Keyframe Timeline provides two sets of Tools and Control buttons in the header.

▶ **Edit Tools**

- **Arrow - edit** keyframes:
  For selecting, creating and editing keyframes
- **Pencil - sketch** keyframes:
  For drawing keyframes
- **Rectangle - transform** keyframes:
  For drawing a selection box to limit the edit to the keyframes inside the box

▶ **Control Buttons**

Please pay attention to the different modes of these buttons. They can trigger a command, have an on/off state or provide a menu.

- **Display Audio Waveform** (menu): This button provides a popup menu that displays all available Audio Objects plus a Master Track that you can choose to make visible in the Graph.
- **Clear Curve List** (command): This is a special command only for the custom Parameter Set. It modifies the currently viewed custom Parameter List by removing all parameters. You can undo the action.
- **Fit Curves** (command): Zooms the Graph vertically and horizontally to fit all the Keyframes (not necessarily the whole length of the Project).
- **Curve Snapshot** (on/off): This button has an on (blue) and off (grey) position. From the moment you activate it, it will remember the state of any curve before you change it. You can use this for two things. First, the "Curve Snapshot" will be visible as a comparison when you edit a parameter. Second, you can revert to this "snapshot curve" with the "Set Curve Snapshot" command from the Animation Menu.
- **Snapping** (on/off): When moving Keyframes, they will line up with other items (keyframes, markers, grid point).
- **Auto-Scale Vertically** (on/off): This will hide the vertical scroll bar and automatically zooms the graph vertically to fit the curves.

▶ **Zoom/Scroll Controls**

- **Horizontal**: The graph can be zoomed horizontally with the zoom slider or the zoom handles on each side of the scroll bar (and also with the 2-finger pinch gesture of a trackpad). These controls affect all three timeline views (Video Timeline, Audio Timeline, Keyframe Timeline) because they share the same timeline after all.
- **Vertical**: Use the vertical scroll bar or the auto-scale mode.

Keyframe Graph

Once we have the correct parameters displayed in the Parameters List, we can view their values in the Graph on the right. All the visible parameters share one single graph (x/y axis). Even though the Parameters are color coded, it makes sense to display only a subset of Parameters at a time to make it easier to view and edit specific curves.

▶ **Appearance**

- Parameters have different colors.
- Keyframes are displayed as diamonds in the color of their parameter. Selected Keyframes are white.
- Interpolation lines (curves) are solid in the color of their parameter. They turn white if the parameter is selected. The line before the first and after the last keyframe is dotted.
- If one Object is selected then the graph will display two vertical white lines that mark the beginning and end of that Object. (No need to create some elaborate curves between 2s and 4s when the Object is only visible between 5s and 10s)
- Project Marker created in any of the three Timelines views are visible to all of them because they share the same Timeline ruler on top.
- The units at the x axis on the left are only displayed if a single Parameter is selected.

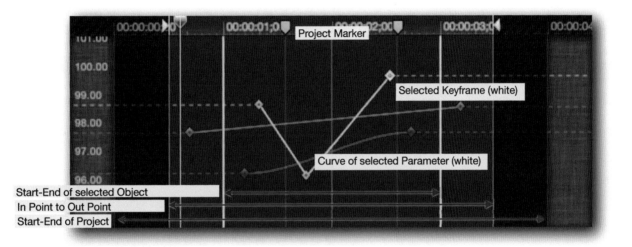

▶ **Editing**

Although the Keyframe Timeline is the best place to view parameter changes over time, creating and editing those parameters via Keyframes can be done in other window elements too like the Inspector, HUD and Canvas. The presence of Keyframes in a parameter can change the behavior how those parameters are edited in specific windows. If the complexity of your Motion Project grows, you better be sure of what happens at every click you make to avoid accidental surprises.

Here is the basic concept again. Window elements are linked when viewing or editing parameters. Changes in one window will be displayed in all the other windows at the same time.

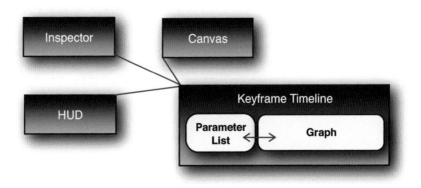

Now I'll try to show the edit behavior in linked windows in these three screenshots. They are a little small to see the details but it is important to get familiar with the big picture on how the windows are simply different views into the same Object or parameter of an Object.

The Object here is a rectangle and the parameter is the Roundness. The red rectangles focus on the control that changes the value in each window. The red circles show the graph in the Keyframe Timeline.

There are two fundamental conditions when it comes to editing parameters.

💡 No Keyframes exist for a parameter

In the first screenshot, there are no Keyframes programmed for the Roundness. Changing the value in any window would change the value simultaneously in the other windows. The Graph displays only a dotted line (indicating a constant value) that would move up or down when you change any of the controls.

💡 One or more Keyframes exist for a parameter

In the second screenshot, I added the first Keyframe. You can do that by clicking the Keyframe button in the Inspector or Parameters list or by creating a Keyframe directly on the dotted line inside the graph.

Visually nothing has changed. The Parameter still stays the same throughout the Project. Even if you change the Parameter with any of the available controls, it is the same behavior. In the graph, the Keyframe would move up or down with the whole line.

However, the fact that one Keyframe now exists, changes how the controller acts. Each parameter with at least one Keyframe changes to the "Initial Keyframe Method" which is indicated by red parameter values.

In the third screenshot, I moved the playhead to a new position and this is how the controllers behave now:

- Moving any parameter controls in any of the windows will automatically create a Keyframe and adjusts its value. That means that the parameter controls now have the added functionality of creating Keyframes and not only changing the value of the parameter. (This is the behavior of the "Initial Keyframe Method").

- Of course you still can create a new Keyframe first and then adjust the value with the controls.

> Please note that the Preview section in the left upper corner of the Inspector will display a thumbnail of the Object that displays the state of the Object at the current playhead position (static only, not during play)

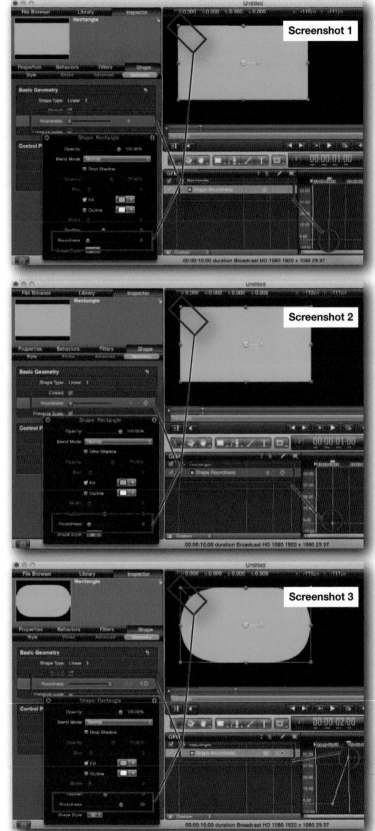

These two behaviors of editing parameters (Keyframe exist vs Keyframe does not exit) are important when we look at what happens when we create Keyframes for a specific parameter.

There are almost too many options on how to add Keyframes. A good approach to understand the complexity of creating and editing Keyframes is to bring it down to two basic questions:

☑ **When** to add Keyframes.
This is a question about the circumstances. Was the Keyframe created for the first time or was one created before? Is that special Keyframe record button activated or deactivated?

☑ **How** to add Keyframes.
What is the procedure, the mechanics, i.e. Click on a specific control in a specific window, etc.

💡 When

There are three possible circumstances in which you might create Keyframes.

A. **No Keyframe** exists yet for that parameter.

B. **At least one Keyframe** exists for that parameter (Initial Keyframe Method).

C. **Record Animation** is active.
You can toggle this mode with the record button in the Canvas navigation controls. It is also available from the Main Menu Object ➤ Animation Record or with the Key Command A.

💡 How

Here is a list with all the different methods on how to create a Keyframe, organized in seven groups.

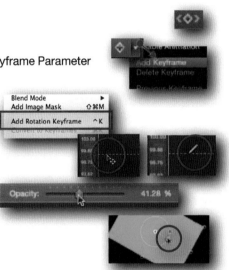

1. **Keyframe Button** in the Inspector or Keyframe Parameter List

2. **Add Keyframe command** from the Animation Menu in the Inspector or Keyframe Parameter List

3. **Main Menu** Object ➤ Add "last modified parameter" Keyframe

4. **Key Command** ctr+K to add Keyframe to the last modified parameter

5. **Keyframe Graph**: Click on a curve with the arrow or pencil tool

6. **Click (move) Control Slider** or change the value in the Inspector or HUD

7. **Click (move) Object** or an Object on-screen control in the Canvas

And these are the combinations:

• **A - No Keyframes exist**:

Method 1-5 can be used. Method 6 and 7 won't create any Keyframe, they only change the value of the parameter.

• **B - Initial Keyframe Method:**

The standard methods 1-5 can be used but also 6 and 7. As we have seen on the previous page, changing controls in the Inspector, HUD or onscreen controls in the Canvas will automatically create a Keyframe under these circumstances. The values in the Inspector are displayed in red to indicate that you are not only changing the value but creating a Keyframe with that value.

• **C - Record Animation:**

This is the same behavior as the Initial Keyframe Method (B). But now, it doesn't matter if a Keyframe exists for the parameter or not. However there is one specialty. When creating the first Keyframe with method 6 or 7 and the playhead is not parked at the beginning, then this will create two Keyframes, one at the playhead position plus a second one at the beginning of the Project.

And if that wouldn't be enough, there is one more aspect when asking the "When" question. Online or Offline?
In automation (and that is what animation is), there are two basic modes for programming the automation.

- **Online**: The playhead is moving while you perform the automation (creating Keyframes)
- **Offline**: The playhead is not moving while you perform the automation (creating Keyframes)

The good news is that online/offline status doesn't have any affect on the behavior we just discussed. Instead, Motion provides a settings window where you can check whether or not you want to enable the creation of Keyframes while the playhead is moving.

You can open the Settings window with any of those commands:

- Main Menu Command **Mark ➤ Recording Options...**
- Key Command **opt+A**
- **double+click** on the Record button

In addition to the checkbox "Don't record keyframes during playback", there are three radio buttons to set the Keyframe Thinning. This will reduce the amount of recorded keyframes to make more use of interpolation curves for smoother transitions.

- *Off*: keep Keyframes as they are.
- *Reduced*: Reduce the density of Keyframes.
- *Peaks Only*: Keep only the Keyframes when the curve is changing directions, everything else is interpolated.

Keyframe Graph Editing

There are a wide variety of commands and techniques on how to create and edit Keyframes in the Graph. But before you do anything, consider two things:

1. Select the Parameter(s) first, either from the Parameters List or by selecting its Curve.
2. Be sure of what you are editing:
   - Keyframe(s)
   - Curve

► **Snapshot**

This is a very helpful feature when making visual changes in the Graph

Instant Curve Snapshot

Whenever you drag a Curve or Keyframes from their position, Motion makes a snapshot of the original curve first so you can see what the original curve was before you start dragging it. This curve will be visible until you release the mouse.

Manual Curve Snapshot

When you turn on the Snapshot mode, the current curve will still be visible (as a guide) no matter how much you alter the curve for that parameter. Turning off the snapshot mode will delete that visual guide. You can even restore the Snapshot curve with the "Set to Curve Snapshot" command from the Animation menu as long as the mode is active.

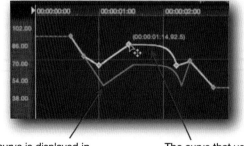

Snapshot curve is displayed in
the color of the Parameter

The curve that you're dragging
at the moment is white

► **Visual Edits**

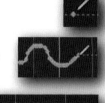

💡 **Add single Keyframe with Edit Tool** (Arrow)

Either opt+click or double+click on the Curve.

💡 **Add single Keyframe with Sketch Tool** (Pencil)

You can click anywhere in the Graph. You can even have multiple Parameters selected.

💡 **Add multiple Keyframes with Sketch Tool** (Pencil)

You can drag the mouse across the Graph to draw a line (even for multiple selected Parameters). The slower the movements, the denser the Keyframes. Any existing Keyframes in the path will be overwritten.

💡 **Change single Keyframe value numerically**

Double+click on a Keyframe will open a little overlay window. The tiny number on top displays the timecode position of the Keyframe and the box lets you enter a new numerical value for the Keyframe.

💡 **Change single/multiple Keyframe graphically** (value/position)

You can drag any Keyframe with the Edit Tool to a new position. This also works with multiple selected Keyframes that don't even have to be next to each other. Motion redraws the curve while you're dragging so you can see the result before you release the mouse. You have to drag one of the selected Keyframes (not the Curve). A little number overlay updates the current position of that Keyframe while you are dragging. Sh+drag restricts to vertical movement.

💡 **Change multiple Keyframes at once - Transform Tool** (Rectangle)

When you drag a selection around some Keyframes with the Transform tool and release the mouse, then the rectangle will snap to the closest Keyframes inside. Now you can treat those enclosed Keyframes graphically:

- Dragging the whole section moves the Keyframes as it is up/down (value) and left/right (position). Sh+drag restricts to one direction (press the shift key before the drag restricts to vertical, press it right after the movement, restricts it to that direction).

- Dragging any of the four side handles stretches or compresses the Keyframe position horizontally, dragging any of the four corner handles stretches or expands their position vertically. Opt+drag moves opposite sides at the same time. Sh+drag keeps the aspect ratio of the selected frame.

- Cmd+drag any of the four corner handles to distort the frame and move the Keyframes inside accordingly.

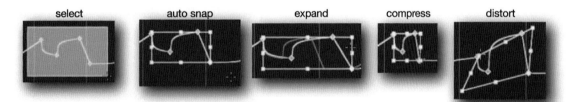

| select | auto snap | expand | compress | distort |

💡 **Change Curve**

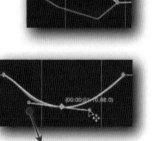

You can drag a line segment (the line between two Keyframes vertically (only). This moves the left and right Keyframe with it and therefore affects the shape of the next curves too.

💡 **Change to a Bezier Curve**

Cmd+drag on a Keyframe transforms it into a Bezier Keyframe. The Bezier handles will appear and let you shape the curve. Sh+drag snaps the tangents to 45 degree.

Opt+drag a handle of a control point to adjust that side independently.

Ctr+click on the control opens a small Shortcut Menu that lets you align both tangents or break them apart for individual adjustment of both tangents.

Cmd+drag on the Bezier Keyframe resets the curve to a linear shape again.

Shortcut Menu

Break Tangent
Align Tangents

▶ **Menu Commands**

Besides visual manipulation by clicking and dragging Keyframes and Curves, you can also use various menus that provide additional commands:

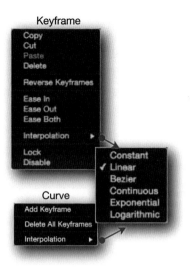

Keyframe

💡 **Keyframe Shortcut Menu**

The following commands affect a single or multiple selected Keyframes: *Cut*, *Copy*, *Paste*, *Delete*, *Lock* (can't modify), *Disable* (grayed out and will be ignored by the curve).

The *Reverse Keyframes* command flips the values of selected Keyframe # (i.e. #1-#2-#3-#4) in reverse order (#4-#3-#2-#1).

Ease In, Ease Out, Ease Both, and the choices from the *Interpolation* submenu affect the curve after and/or before the Keyframe.

💡 **Curve Shortcut Menu**

Add a Keyframe at the position of the Curve that you clicked.

Delete All Keyframes for that parameter.

Select the curve type from the same *Interpolation* submenu.

💡 **Animation Menu**

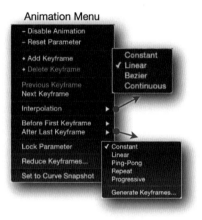

I explained the commands for the Animation Menu a few pages earlier in the Parameter List section. I just want to point out that all the commands in this menu affect all their Keyframes and the resulting curves for the selected Parameter.

▶ **Save Curves**

We learned in the Chapter about the Library Pane that you could save your custom Objects to the Motion Library so you can have access to them regardless what Project you are in (or exchange them with other users). You can do the same with Curves:

Let's say you created a special curve for a bouncy ball. All you have to do now is select those Parameters that make up the movement in the Parameters List and drag them back to the Library window into the Stack of the Favorites folder (maybe rename it for better identification afterwards). From now on, whatever Project you are in, you can drag that Curve directly onto an Object and the Keyframes for that parameter will be applied to it.

You can drag one Parameter or multiple Parameters into the Library. In the later case, an overlay lets you choose if you want to save them as one or individual curves.

As with other Library Objects, the curve will be available as a Motion Library Object (.molo). See the Library chapter for details.

▶ **Behavior vs Keyframes**

Behaviors are computer generated movements that are based on algorithms. On the other hand, Keyframes are manually programmed. So the way they are generated is different, but technically they can be represented by the same graph. They are actually displayed in the Keyframe Graph without the option to directly edit them (no Keyframe nodes).

However the Menu Command Object ➤ Convert to Keyframes or Key Command cmd+K converts any movement generated by an assigned Behavior effect into Keyframes and removes the Behavior after the conversion. An alert window reminds you about the limitations of that command

Behavior ─────────────────────────── ➤ Keyframes

Do you want to convert all behaviors of this object to keyframes?

Only behaviors that are applied to and directly affect the selected objects will create keyframes. Behaviors that affect other objects will not be changed.

Cancel   Convert

7 - Canvas

Finally, we get to the last major component in the Motion interface, the Canvas.

No doubt that this is also the most important element, the visual workspace of your Project, where you can see how your Composition is shaping up. This is the only window pane that cannot be hidden. It even has its own command to expand its window pane to the full Motion workspace, hiding every other window element (ctrl+V)

Please note that the Canvas has two purposes:

☑ Lay out and arrange your Objects in the 2D or 3D space and edit them with onscreen controls.

☑ Play your composition and watch the result as you build your Project.

As we know by now, the building blocks of your Composition consist of a wide variety of Objects. Here again is the diagram that emphasizes on the main concept in Motion regarding those Objects.

- You work on one single Composition at a time.
- You add/create Objects to/in that Composition.
- The different windows provide different views to look at those Objects and manipulate them.
  - **Inspector / HUD**: Edit the parameters of an Object.
  - **Project Pane**: Stack the Objects in a specific hierarchy.
  - **Timing Pane**: Manipulate the Objects and most of their parameters over time.
  - **Canvas**: Position the Objects in the 2D or 3D space.
- Play your Composition in the Canvas

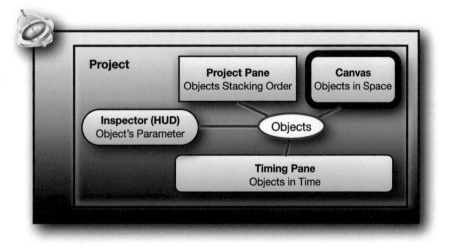

So whatever you do in Motion, you work on Objects through one of these windows depending on what aspect of that Object you want to manipulate. Some processes can be performed in more than one window, so you can choose which one fits your workflow the best.

Add Objects

Think about it, even when you add Objects to your Project, you are not adding them to the "Project". There is no separate Project window". Instead, you can choose from the three different views of your Project (Project Pane, Timing Pane, Canvas), and that is where you add your Objects to as part of your Project.

Create Objects

However, when you want to create a new Object (Shape or Text), you can do that only in the Canvas with the available tools (see the next chapter for details).

Interface

The elements in the Canvas pane are laid out very well.

- 💡 At the top is the context sensitive Status Bar and the five popup menus that configure the appearance of the Canvas.
- 💡 In the center is the main area containing the video frame of your Project, your Composition.
- 💡 At the bottom are three rows: Timeline Ruler, mini-Timeline and Control strip with the Navigation controls and other control buttons

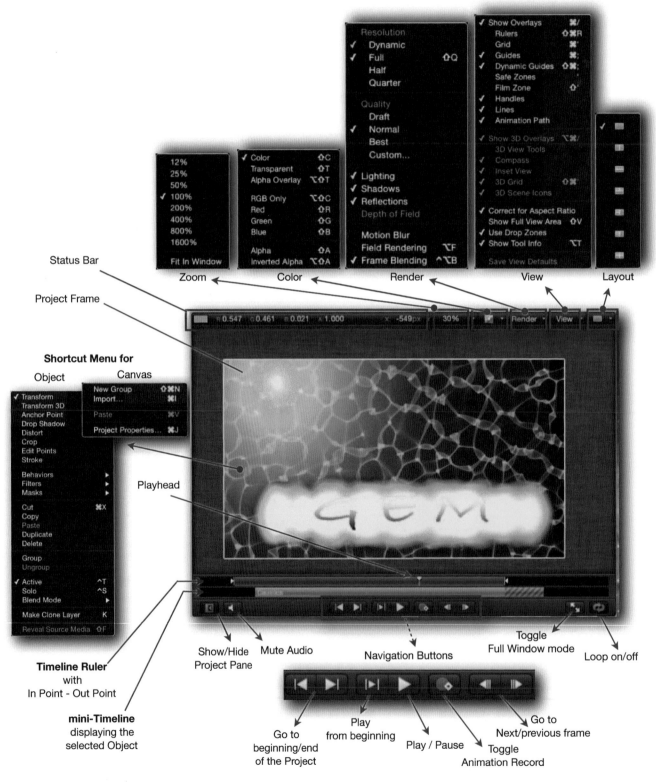

Player Mode

The little tooltip window displays "Full Screen" and not "Player Mode" when you move the mouse over that button. This explains its function better than the generic term *Player Mode*. What happens is that the Canvas takes over the whole Motion window, hiding any other visible window pane (except the Toolbar). So it's not really a full computer screen mode either.

For an additional full screen view use the Menu Command Window ➤ Zoom

Player Mode can also be toggled with the Menu Command Window ➤ Player Mode or the Key Command F8.

The Canvas can also be displayed on a second computer screen. This includes the Project Pane too, because they share the same logical window pane. Use the Menu Command Window ➤ Show Canvas on Second Display.

Navigation

▶ **Navigation Button**

The Navigation buttons are standard. The same controls plus a few more are also available through Key Commands or from the Mark Menu.

▶ **Timeline**

The Canvas even has its own timeline, fairly simple but very effective.

- There are two timeline bars.
- The length of the bars from left to right always represent the length of your Composition.
- There is no time ruler. However, when you move anything on the timeline, the timing information will be displayed in the Time Display below or in a tooltip window overlay.
- The top bar displays the Playhead and the In Point and Out Point that define the Loop range. You can drag them across the timeline with the mouse.
- The bar below, called the mini-Timeline, displays the Object (Layer or Group) that is currently selected. Because the length of the mini-Timeline represents the total length of your Project, it is easy to see when the selected Object is visible in your Composition.

▶ **Time Display**

The popup menu on the Time Display has two modes:

- Display SMPTE or Frames
- Display the duration of the Project or the current Playhead position. The clock icon changes its appearance

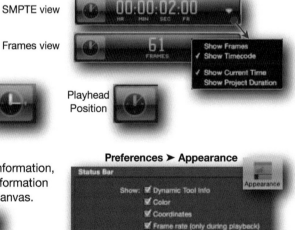

▶ **Status Bar**

This section in the upper left corner of the Canvas provides dynamic information, i.e. the position coordinates of an Object that you drag, or the Color information of your Project when you move your mouse to different spots on the Canvas.

You can configure what kind of information is displayed by selecting the various checkboxes in the Preferences ➤ Appearance ➤ Status Bar window.

Canvas View Menus

There are 5 popup menus that let you configure the appearance of the Canvas.

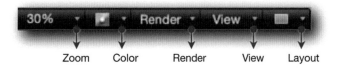

Zoom   Color   Render   View   Layout

► Zoom Level Menu

Before setting the zoom level, make sure to understand the different sizes:

- **Size of the Canvas**: This is the size of the window pane. You can resize with the standard window controls (drag the lower right corner of your window).

- **Size of the Project Frame**: This is the actual size of the video frame of your Project (its resolution), what you see when you export your Project and watch it in the Quicktime player.

- **Size of an Object**: Keep in mind that an Object can be bigger (or grow bigger) than the actual Project Frame. The outline would extend into the Canvas area but only the portion inside the Project frame will be visible. (except when "*Show Full View Area*" is enabled in the View menu)

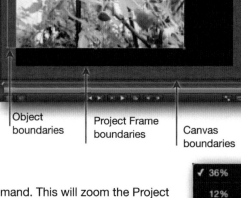

Object boundaries   Project Frame boundaries   Canvas boundaries

The various Zoom levels in this popup menu change the view of the Project Frame to zoom into a section and make finer adjustments on an Object. The size of the Canvas is not affected.

The menu provides eight default zoom levels plus the *Fit In Window* command. This will zoom the Project Frame to fit into the available Canvas.

You can use the pinch gesture on a trackpad to zoom in (and out) to any level, or use the Key command cmd+minus or cmd+equal. (**View ► Zoom Out**, **View ► Zoom In**). In that case, the current zoom level (other than the default values) is displayed on top of the default values. Use the Key Command opt+Z to zoom to 100%

► Color Channels Menu

This menu lets you select which color channels are displayed. The same commands are also available in the Main Menu **View ► Channels ►**.

The term *Background* describes the area in your Project Frame that is not covered by a Layer Object.

- *Color*: Displays the Background in the color set in the Project Properties.
- *Transparent*: Displays the Background as a checkerboard pattern (only if the Project Properties is set to Transparent).
- *Alpha Overlay*: Displays the Background as a red color.
- "*individual channels*": The other settings let you select individual channels. The menu icon in the Canvas changes accordingly to show what is selected.

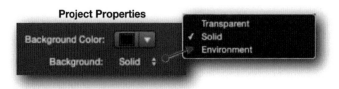

► **Render Menu**

All the computer-generated objects and effects in your Project have to be - that's right - generated by a computer. This process of doing the necessary calculations is called "rendering". Your CPU has to calculate everything in real time and the more objects and effect you add, the more work the CPU has to perform. Depending on how powerful your computer is, it will reach a point where it struggles to get all the calculations properly done in time.

The different options in this menu let you set compromises. You can trade how good the computer-generated quality of your Project looks in the Canvas for a smoother operation by your computer. The "*Custom...*" settings opens a window that provides more detailed settings. Please note that this affects only the viewing of your Project in the Canvas not the render quality when you export your Project.

The commands in this popup menu are also available in the Main Menu under
View ➤ Resolution ➤ , View ➤ Quality ➤ , View ➤ Render Options ➤

- *Resolution*: Sets the displayed resolution between Full, Half and Quarter. In addition to that, the *Dynamic* settings lowers the image quality during playback, scrubbing or when you modify Objects in the Canvas.
- *Quality*: Sets the different levels of render quality.
- *Render Options*: This section lets you disable (uncheck) various elements in your Project that have a high CPU demand.

► **View and Overlay Menu**

This menu lets you enable visual guides and controls that are added to the canvas. Of course, they are not part of your exported Project.

All those options are also available in the Main Menu View ➤

Most of the menu items are self explanatory or you can toggle them to see what they are. Here are a few that might need further explanation:

- *Show Overlay*: This enables/disables all the selected Overlays below, like a master switch.
- *Guides / Dynamic Guides*

  Motion distinguishes between two types of Guides:

  - **Dynamic Guides**: These can be any border of an existing Object or its position in the canvas. In addition, they can be any symmetrical lines of your canvas (center, half, etc), anything you might want an Object align to.
  - **Guides**: These are manual Guides that you can create freely on your canvas as a reference to align Objects to.

    You can enable snap mode with the Menu Command View ➤ Snap or Key Command N so Objects will snap to any of those guides. Holding down the command key disables the Guides and snapping until you release the key again. Please note that this snap mode is independent from the snap mode in the Timing Pane.

Create Guides

You create Guides by dragging from the upper left corner of the Canvas. Dragging on the horizontal ruler creates a vertical guide, dragging on the vertical ruler creates a horizontal line. Dragging onto the Canvas will create both lines with the crossing point at the cursor position. A little info box displays the coordinates.

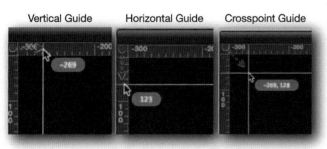

Vertical Guide   Horizontal Guide   Crosspoint Guide

You can move an existing Guide by dragging the line in the ruler area. Dragging it all the way back to the left upper corner will delete it in a "puff of smoke".

The Ruler has to be visible for those operations.

The Main Menu **View** ➤ **Guides** ➤ opens a submenu containing additional commands for Guides like Lock, Clear and Add.

Canvas Preferences

The Canvas tab in the Preferences window provides many controls and menus to customize the behavior and look of those overlays.

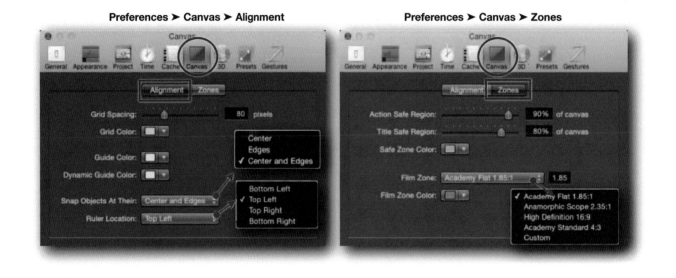

Preferences ➤ Canvas ➤ Alignment   **Preferences ➤ Canvas ➤ Zones**

- The 3D related menu items are only available when you work in 3D mode. I cover those in the 3D Chapter.
- *Correct for Aspect Ratio*: This compensates the Aspect Ratio for pixels and only affects the Canvas, not the exported Project.
- *Show Full View Area*: This makes the portion of an Object Layer visible if it extends outside the visible Project frame. Disable it to save unnecessary CPU activity.

- *Use Drop Zones*: If you are using a special Drop Zone Object in your Project, then this lets you drag Objects onto it.
- *Show Tool Info*: This enables an overlay that displays the Control Point Number when you mouse over a Control Point of a shape.
- *Save View Defaults*: Saves the state of the above setting of this menu when you launch Motion.

➤ **Layout Menu**

This menu lets you divide the Canvas area to have the Project frame not only displayed once, but multiple times in various screen arrangements. Please note that all those frames (viewports) display the same single Project you are working on. However, all the Canvas options from the menus we just discussed, can be set differently for each displayed frame.

Click on a Frame to select it, it will have a yellow border around it. Only the selected frame will be active and play your Composition when you hit play.

Those multi-view layouts are especially useful when working in 3D mode to display different camera view points.

8 - Tools

Now that we covered all the three window elements that let you view and work on your Project (plus window number 4, the Inspector), let's step back and pick up on the earlier Chapter about adding Objects to your Project.

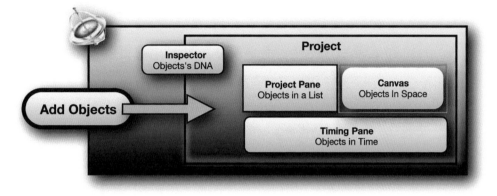

There are two ways to add new Objects to your Project:

Adding Existing Objects

Media files or computer-generated graphics from the Motion Library or your hard drive.

Create New Objects

Motion provides tools that let you create new Objects from scratch.

In this chapter, we concentrate on the tools for creating new Objects and the tools to edit Objects.

The first place to look for tools is, of course, the always visible Toolbar. The two groups of buttons on the far right are for adding Objects to the Project and adding Objects (Filters, Behaviors) to other Objects. However, we are interested now in the two groups on the left: Editing Objects and Creating Objects.

What are Tools?

A tool is represented by a button on the user interface that you click to select a specific functionality. This changes not only the appearance and function of the mouse cursor but also onscreen controls in the Canvas. By selecting a different button (or through Key Commands), you switch between those tools depending on what kind of task you want to perform next. Those different tools are required when editing Objects directly in the Canvas via onscreen controls instead of entering just parameter values in the Inspector.

It is always important to be aware of what the current selected tool is so you know what happens when you click or drag items. Keep an eye on the selected tool button (blue) and look for the (dynamically) changing type of cursor. But also pay attention to how the onscreen controls change their appearance (handles, control points, lines, etc).

❶ Tools to Edit Objects

These are the different Tools that are mainly used in the Canvas for on-screen controls. This is a highly visual and direct way to interact with the actual Object instead of entering numbers in the Inspector and figuring out how that will change the appearance of the Object in the Canvas.

❷ Tools to Create Objects

These Tools let you use the mouse as a drawing tool to create different kind of Objects. If you use those Tools a lot, then a Graphics tablet might be more suitable than a mouse.

Edit Tools

This group has three buttons, two function as a popup menu with more tools inside. The tools are object sensitive, which means that they are only selectable when they provide functionality for the currently selected Object. Otherwise, they are grayed out.

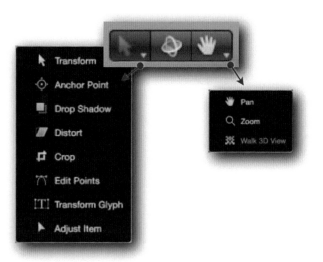

You can perform any edits while you're playing your Composition (in loop mode) so you can see changes right away.

Instead of just listing all the tools and describing what they do, I'll add a screenshot of the Canvas to show how the onscreen controls change with the tool. The onscreen controls are a visual equivalent of the actual parameter values. That's why I think it is important to also have a screenshot of the Inspector module to show what parameter value(s) are affected by altering an Object visually.

And one more thing. The different tools change the functionality of the mouse cursor mainly in the Canvas for the onscreen controls. Using the mouse in other parts of the interface works as usual. You can still select items or change values regardless of the selected tool.

2D Transform

The first button is a popup menu that contains eight different tools, mainly for altering 2D Objects.

The Key Command access is a little bit strange.

- The Key Command **S** selects the currently visible Tool in the Toolbar. This is the one that was last selected from the menu.

- After that, use the **Tab** key to step through the 8 Tools. But somehow the second button to the right, the *3D Transform* tool, is also included in the sequence (after the Transform tool). When the 3D Transform tool was last selected and you use the Key Command **S**, it will select this tool (even if it has its own Key Command **Q**). Maybe a bit confusing.
  Sequence: Transform - **3D Transform** (!) - Anchor Point - Drop Shadow - Distort - Crop - Edit Points - Transform Glyph - Adjust Item

- **Sh+Tab** will step backwards through the menu.

- **Sh+S** switches directly to the Transform tool without stepping through the cycle

- **Double+click** on that tool button will also switch directly to the default Transform tool.

This is the default tool. The Object handles are blue circles.

Inspector ➤ Properties ➤ Transform

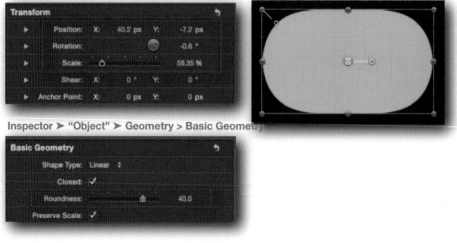

- **Position**: Drag the Object around.

- **Rotation**: Drag the rotation handle. The further you drag away from the center, the finer the adjustments. **Sh+drag** restricts to increments of 45° angles.

- **Scale**: Drag the handles. Use the **sh+drag** to restrict the aspect ratio and **opt+drag** to move both sides at once.

Inspector ➤ "Object" ➤ Geometry > Basic Geometry

- **Roundness**: Drag the little handle in the left upper corner to change the Roundness. This parameter is located in the Geometry tab

Anchor Point

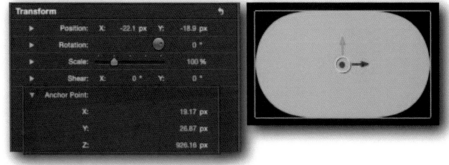

When selected, an onscreen control appears for the selected Object that lets you **drag** the Anchor Point in any direction (X, Y, Z). The anchor point is used as the rotation and scaling point for an Object.

- **Anchor Point (X, Y, Z)**: The coordinates represent an offset value from the Object's center point. Please note that the absolute coordinates for the Anchor Point are identical to the coordinates of the Position value (see below for further details).

Drop Shadow

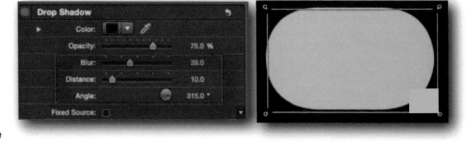

The Object handles are little circles.

Dragging any of the four corner handles away from the objects increases the Blur value.

Dragging the object will move the white frame (not the object). This changes the Distance and Angle of the shadow at the same time.

- **Blur**: Please not that you can set the Blur in the Inspector only to 100 maximum. The onscreen controls on the Canvas lets you drag even further.
- **Distance / Angle**: Dragging the frame correlates to the distance (from the Object) and the angle (0° to the right, 90° up, 180° left, etc).

Distort

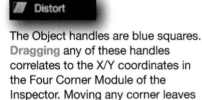
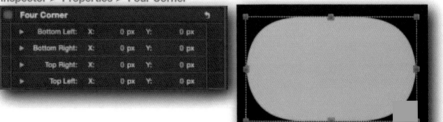

The Object handles are blue squares. **Dragging** any of these handles correlates to the X/Y coordinates in the Four Corner Module of the Inspector. Moving any corner leaves the other three corners fixed, which distorts the Object's geometry.

Sh+drag the side handles restricts the movement to horizontal or vertical.

- **Bottom Left - Bottom Right - Top Left - Top Right**

Crop

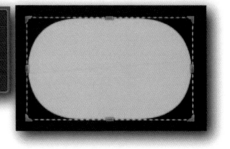

The Object handles are blue triangles and rectangles.

You can crop either side

Sh+drag keeps the aspect ratio.

Opt+drag also moves the opposite side.

- **Left - Right - Bottom - Top**

Edit Points

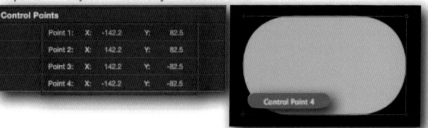

The Edit Points tool displays red handles in the Canvas. These are the "Control Points". (That's why the tool is called "Edit Points", makes sense?)

Double+click on a shape switches to the Edit Point Tool regardless which Tool was selected.

Moving the mouse over a Control Point changes the cursor to a cross and a little window pops up displaying the number of that Control Point.

You can create more Control Points by **opt+click** on the outline of the shape (the cursor changes to a quill pen). The new Point will be displayed right away in the Inspector. The numbering is dynamically updated, always from the first to the last Point.

Another speciality is the Contextual Menu when you **ctr+click** on a Control Point. These extended commands are not available in the Inspector.

 **Transform Glyph**

This tool is only available for a Text Object. It Is a 3D Transform tool.

Although you edit the text Object as a whole (the whole word or phrase), this tool lets you manipulate an individual character or group of characters (the currently selected ones).

See the 3D Chapter for details about how to use 3D onscreen controls.

- **Scale**: Dragging any of the 8 handles changes the size of the character.
- **Offset**: Dragging the selected character will move it (offset it) from its original position.
- **Rotation**: Use any of the three rotational axes (green, red, blue) to rotate the character in the 3D space.

▶ **Adjust Item**

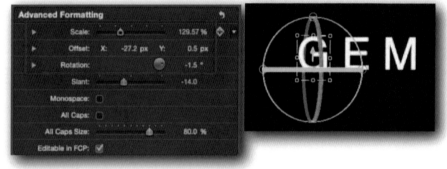

The Adjust Item tool isn't linked to a specific module in the Inspector or a specific type of onscreen control. It varies with the Object or Parameter. The tool activates onscreen controls that allow you to manipulate a variety of parameters of an Object like Filters, Behaviors, Generators, and other Objects. For example, adjust the center point of a blur filter, the settings of a gradient, or the shape of a particle emitter.

The screenshot to the right shows an example of the Behavior Motion path.

Here is an overview of all the eight Tools and the modules in the Inspector they are referring to.

Just an example

3D Transform

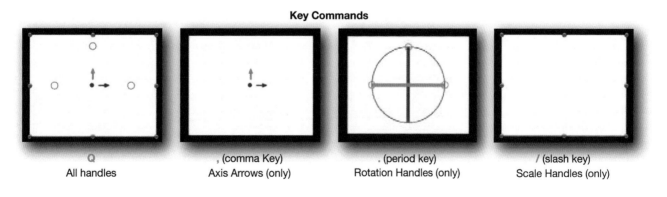

3D Transform Tool

The 3D Transformation tool can be used in 2D or 3D spaces. When active, the selected Object will display three types of onscreen handles. The screenshot below shows a white rectangle as the selected Object with the onscreen controls.

- 🔵 **Scale Handles**: These are the same eight blue handles as with the 2D Transform tool.
- 🔵 **Axis Arrows**: Each axes is represented by a colored arrow: X=red, Y=green, Z=blue. The blue arrow looks like a dot because it points straight at you. Dragging any arrow will move the Object on that axis. Dragging the blue Z-axis works only if the Object is part of 3D Group.
- 🔵 **Rotation Handle**: These handles look like white circles that turn into rotation rings when clicked on. They let you rotate the Object around any of the three axis.

Besides using the **S** key and stepping through the sequence of the 2D Tools, you can use the Key Command **Q** to access the 3D Transform tool directly. In addition to that, there are three more commands that let you toggle between specific viewing modes. They decide which handles are displayed, one type of handles or all three types.

Key Commands

Q	, (comma Key)	. (period key)	/ (slash key)
All handles	Axis Arrows (only)	Rotation Handles (only)	Scale Handles (only)

Here is an example that demonstrates the Rotation Handles. It might get a little bit complicated:

- **Z-axis (blue)**: When you click on the right rotation handle, a blue circle appears. This is the rotation path when moving the Object around the Z-axis. Please note that the Z-axis is the Anchor Point which you also can move with the Anchor Tool. Rotating around the Z-axis is the same as rotating the Rotation Handle with the 2D transform tool.

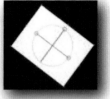

Click here, selects the Z-axis

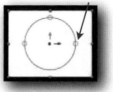

Rotates around the Z-axis

- **X-axis (red)**: When you click on the top rotation handle, a thick red line appears. This might be confusing at first because the X-axis is indicated by the (still visible) red arrow. This arrow represents the X-axis and the thick red line is actually the rotation path around that X-axis. You're just looking straight at it and that's why it appears to be a line.

Click here, selects the X-axis

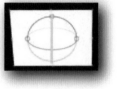

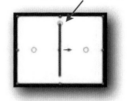

Rotates around the X-axis

- **Y-axis (green)**: When you click on the left rotation handle, a thick green line appears. The same thing happens here. The still visible green arrow represents the Y-axis and the thick green line is the rotation path around the Y-axis when looking straight at it.
A rotation line turns yellow when you "use" it, rotate the Object around that axis.

Click here, selects the Y-axis

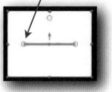

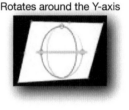

Rotates around the Y-axis

There is one special Key Command combination:

Selecting the 3D Transform tool displays the three axis arrows ❶. Moving the mouse over any of the arrows and holding down the **command** key will change the display to show all three rotation paths ❷. Now keep the command key pressed. **Dragging** over any of the rotation paths will rotate only that axis. However, (still holding the command key) **dragging** anywhere else will let you rotate freely around all the axis with the movement of your mouse. ❸

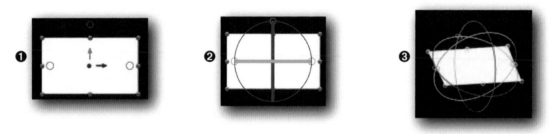

Inspector ➤ Properties ➤ Transform

Please note that regardless of how complex the 3D movement of your Object will be, all that data is represented by the X, Y and Z values of the Position, Rotation and Scale parameters in the Transform module of the Inspector. The same parameters are displayed in the Timing Pane when you record Keyframes for animation of the Object.

As we have learned before, this is a typical example that shows how the three panes (Project Pane, Timing Pane, Canvas) display your Composition, just with a different view.

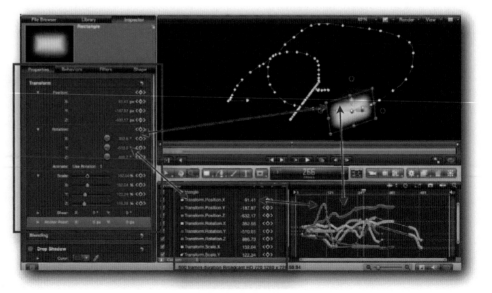

3D HUD

There is one additional "side effect" of the 3D Transform tool. Switching to the 3D Transform Tool will also change the HUD. It will have now additional 3D tools at the bottom.

Dragging on any of the five buttons will let you move the selected Object, in 3D space.

This becomes very powerful because you can record those mouse movements as keyframes.

View Tools

The Project frame is usually centered in the Canvas. However, you can move the Project frame around with this tool without affecting any of the Objects inside the frame.

- Key Command H selects the Pan tool
- Drag with the Pan tool to position the Project frame on the Canvas.
- Space+drag to position the Project frame with just the Arrow tool (no need to switch to the Pan tool).
- Double+click on the Pan tool in the toolbar to reset the frame position back to the center.

Zoom

It is important where to click. This is the point where you zoom in to or zoom out from, like a center point of your zoom. That point is marked with a cross while you drag the mouse.

- Key Command Z selects the Zoom tool
- Drag right-left: zoom in-out
- Click: zooms in by 50%
- Opt+click: zooms out by 50%
- Double+click on the Zoom tool in the toolbar resets to 100% zoom

Walk 3D View

This is a tool for working in 3D space. When a Camera is selected in the Layers list, this mode lets you move that camera in the 3D space with the arrow keys or the mouse similar to video game controllers. (holding the option key will move the Camera more slowly).

For Scene cameras, you can use this control mode to record its movement as keyframes.

See the 3D Chapter for more details.

Create Tools

Next to the Edit Tools are the buttons for the Create Tools. Three of them function as popup buttons to select more tools from a menu.

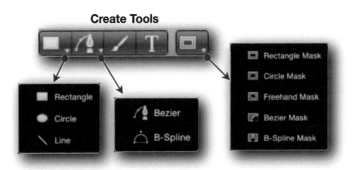

What looks like a big variety of Objects that you can create, actually represents only two kinds of Objects. *Text* and *Shape*.

Instead of explaining how to create all those "different" Objects, I want to first show why there are only two kinds. Once you understand their differences (or what they have in common), then it will be much easier to learn how to create them.

First, let me organize the tools in a table to get a basic overview.

- 💡 **Text**: There is only one tool to create a Text Object.
- 💡 **Shape**: There are six types of Shapes and five types of a special kind of Shape, the *Shape Mask*. Shapes and Shape Masks differ mainly in their functionality in the Project Layer. Regarding the creation and their geometry, they work the same as their equivalent Shape counterparts.

	Shape	key			**Shape Mask**	key
	Rectangle	R			Rectangle Mask	opt+R
	Circle	C			Circle Mask	opt+C
	Line					
	Bezier	B			Bezier Mask	opt+B
	B-Spline	B			B-Spline Mask	opt+B
	Paint Stroke	P			Freehand Mask	opt+P
	Text	key				
	Text	T				

A few things to pay attention to:

- The Key Command for each Tool is easy to remember with their first letter. The Shape Masks use the same key with the added option key.
- The Bezier tool and the B-Spline tool share the same key command. They function as a toggle. Every time you press again, you select the other one.
- The Paint Stroke tool in the Shape section and the Freehand Mask in the Shape Mask section share the same letter because creating a shape with a "Paint Stroke" is just another term for creating a shape with "Freehand".

8 - Tools

Basics

In order to explain how to create a simple shape, let's do a little detour into math territory to review some basics.

Every 2-dimensional Shape is defined by two basic parameters:

- 💡 **Control Points**. The x, y coordinates.
- 💡 **Lines**: the lines that connects from one control point to the next control point.

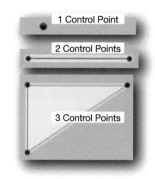

About Control Points:

- 1 Control Point: A shape with only one control point is only a coordinate (without a line)
- 2 Control Points: A shape with two Control Points is a line segment, a one-dimensional shape.
- 3 or more Control Points: At least three Control Points are necessary to create a 2-dimensional shape.

About Lines

The lines that connect the Control Points can have different forms:

- *Linear Line*: This is the most simple form when you draw a straight line between the Control Points.
- *Bezier Curve*: Here, the line between the Control Points is curved based on a specific mathematical function. Instead of entering values into a complex formula to manipulate the shape of the curve, graphics applications like Motion provide easy to use onscreen handles that let you manipulate the curve visually.
- *B-Spline Curve*: Here, the line between the Control Points is also curved, based on a different mathematical function. Again, instead of entering values, onscreen handles lets you manipulate the curve. What's special about this curve is that the curve doesn't go through the Control Points.
- *Roundness*: Another onscreen parameter that lets you manipulate the corners of a shape. It curves the lines at a Control Point to form more rounded edges. This control affects all corners equally!

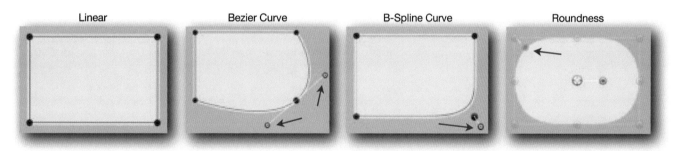

Linear   Bezier Curve   B-Spline Curve   Roundness

💡 **Fill - Outline**

Independent from its geometry, a shape requires at least one of those two attributes. Outline the shape or fill its enclosed area..

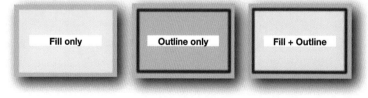

💡 **Open/Closed Shape**

The Control Points that make up a shape are numbered in a sequential order. There is always a first and a last Point. When you connect the last point to the first one, you have a closed shape. If not, then you have an open shape that is relevant when you are using Outlines and some other operations.

Inspector - Shape

Now lets look at the Motion interface to see where those parameters are located that define a shape.

💡 **Object Type**: First, we look in the Inspector at the fourth tab ❶. This is the tab that changes its name, displaying the type of Object that is currently selected. This tab will display "Shape", for every Object that we create with any of the six tools (Rectangle, Circle, Line, Bezier, B-Spline, Paint Stroke). This would support my theory that those tools create the same type of Object, just with different parameters.

The Shape Object is the only Object (besides the Text Object and the Project Object) that has additional sub-tabs in the Inspector.

Geometry tab

Although the last tab, it is the most important because it contains all the parameters that defines the basic attributes of the shape.

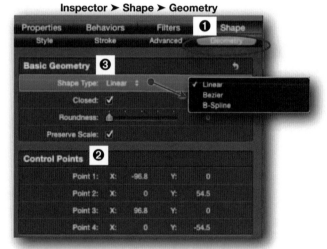

Inspector ➤ Shape ➤ Geometry

▶ **Control Points ❷**

On the previous page, I stated that each shape is defined by two parameters, the Control Points and the Connecting Lines. In the Geometry section, you find the first parameters:

💡 **Control Points**: This is the list of the Control Points and their X/Y coordinates. The more Control Points a Shape has, the longer that list gets.

Attention:

> The X/Y coordinates for the Control Points are not related to your Composition grid!

For example, if you create three different square shapes in your Project frame (upper left corner, lower left corner and center far right) and they all have the same dimensions 200x200, then the Control Point coordinates for all three Shapes would be identical, p1(-100,100) p2(-100,-100) p3(100,-100) p4(100,100).

The reason for that is that the coordinates for the Control Points define the shape itself, independent from the placement in the Project frame of the current Composition. It is like placing the Object in a surrounding frame with the center point at the crossing of an x and y axis (x=0, y=0)

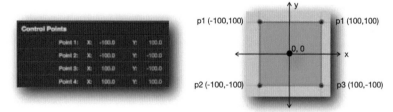

▶ **Basic Geometry ❸**

This module contains the settings for the second parameters, the connecting lines.

💡 **Shape Type**: This is the parameter that defines the type of line that connects the Control Points. A popup menu provides three choices. It is important to understand that this doesn't affect the Control Points, only the shape of the lines/curves that connect the Control Points.

- You can switch freely between the three Shape Types. They even remember any manipulation that you performed with the onscreen handles.

- Please note that the onscreen controls can also switch the selection. If it is set to Linear and you change one corner of a shape with a Bezier onscreen control, then the popup menu changes to Bezier.

💡 **Closed**: The checkbox connects the last Control Point with the first Control Point.

💡 **Roundness**: As I mentioned before, this slider affects all corners in the current shape. It can also be used on Paint Stroke lines to smooth out the edges.

Styles tab

This sub-tab contains the Fill ❶ and Outline ❷ modules with their various parameters plus a Shape Style popup menu ❸ at the top.

The most important parameter is the Brush Type in the Outline module which has some consequences. It provides a popup menu with three options ❹ that determine what is used to draw the outline of the shape.

➤ **Fill**

There is one unique thing about this module. Depending on whether it is on or off, it affects the icon in the Layers list for this Object. If on ❺, the icon looks like a shape with Bezier controls and if the module is off ❻, then the icon changes to a brush indicating that you use the Object as an outline.

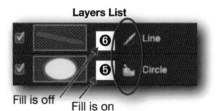

Layers List

Fill is off   Fill is on

➤ **Outline**

The Outline module has a wide variety of parameters available. This is due to the fact that you can get extremely creative with just the outline of shapes or complex freeform lines. Remember, even when drawing lines for illustrations, they are technically just shapes.

The first parameter is the important one:

💡 **Brush Type ❹**

💡 **Solid**: A solid color is used for the outline.

💡 **Airbrush**: Please note that this option will automatically turn off the Fill module!
The available parameters in the Outline module are changing to configure the Airbrush type. The Brush Profiles popup menu ❼ lets you select different presets and you can also save your own settings as custom presets.

💡 **Image**: With this option, you can use any image as the source to "draw" the outline. This opens up endless possibilities beyond the basic creation of a shape. Please note that this option will also turn off the Fill module!
You can drag any Image Layer images from the Project Layer list directly onto the Brush Source image well ❽. Any Layer like Image Sequences, QuickTime movies, Text, and Shapes can be used as a brush source.

When Airbrush or Image is selected, the two other sub-tabs "Stroke" and "Advanced" will become active, providing even more parameters to tweak those Brush Types.

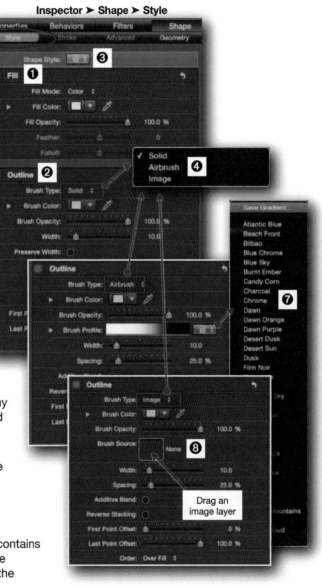

Inspector ➤ Shape ➤ Style

Drag an image layer

💡 **Shape Style ❸**

This popup menu on top of the Fill module contains presets for the Fill/Outline modules. They are organized in themes and most of them use the Images Brush Type.

The last two presets in the list ❾ switch the Brush Type back to Solid or Airbrush.

You can even save your own Shape Style presets.

Here is the list again with all the six Shape tools and their default settings. Think of these different tools as presets with a specific parameter set that is applied when you create a shape with that tool.

	Shape	Geometry (Control Points)	Geometry (Shape Type)	Closed	Fill (on/off)	Outline (Brush Type)
	Rectangle	4	Linear	closed	on	Solid
	Circle	4	Bezier	closed	on	Solid
	Line	2	Linear	open		Solid
	Bezier	(User defined)	Linear	(User defined)	on	Solid
	B-Spline	(User defined)	B-Spline	(User defined)	on	Solid
	Paint Stroke	(User defined)	Bezier	(User defined)		Solid

Here are a few things to pay attention to:

- A circle is nothing other than a shape with four control points where the lines are Bezier Curves.
- With the Bezier and B-Spline tool, you create as many Control Points as you want by clicking on the Canvas. Clicking on the first Control Point at the end will "close" that Shape.
- With the Paint Stroke, you can also create as many Control Points you want. However, instead of creating each single Control Point with a click, you drag (draw) a line and Motion creates the Control Points necessary to define that line. Those freehand strokes are re-calculated as Bezier Curves when you draw curves instead of straight lines.
- The Bezier tool does not create a Bezier Shape Type by default. The lines between the Control Points are Linear. Once you adjust the first corner (cmd+drag on a Control Point), the Shape will then change to Bezier.
- The Fill module is off by default for the Line and Paint Stroke. Makes sense, because you are intend to draw lines and not two-dimensional shapes.
- The Brush Type is always Solid for all the Shape Types. You can switch to Airbrush or Image, but keep in mind that this will turn the Fill module off (if it was activated).

8 - Tools

Three Groups of Parameters

When you are manipulating shapes (and other Objects) in your Composition, you have an overwhelming amount of available parameters that you can tweak either by directly changing their numeric values in the Inspector (the mathematical approach) or indirectly by using onscreen controls in the Canvas (the visual approach), which automatically alters their corresponding numeric values.

With all those parameters, it is easy to get lost even in a mildly complex Project. As I mentioned at the beginning, your Project can get very complicated very fast. In general, when dealing with a big number of items, it is a good idea to group them together or create a hierarchy. Same with parameters. It gives you a better understanding and awareness of any connections or relationships between the parameters. And that's exactly what I'm trying to do now. Group the main parameters into three groups.

The main Parameters of an Object in your Composition can be organized into three groups:

- ☑ Defining the Object
- ☑ Placing the Object
- ☑ Altering the Object (optional)

➡ Defining The Object

This is the first stage, the raw Object. At this point you are doing basic prep work, kind of isolated from its function in the actual Composition. All the parameters in the "Object" tab of the Inspector belong to this group. Those parameters manipulate the Object (Shape, Text, Image, etc) itself.

The most parameters in this group are available for Shape and Text Objects, because they are computer-generated objects where all their individual parameters are created (and altered) in real time. For example, an image (based on a media file) that displays a circle and a text cannot be altered so it shows a triangle and and a different text font.

The most important (and potentially confusing) parameters in this group are the Control Points and their coordinates.

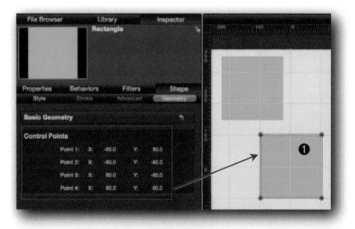

Early on in this chapter, I emphasized that the X/Y coordinates for the Control Points are not related to your Composition grid. Here is an example with two screenshots:

This Project has two squares with the dimensions 160x160.

Screenshot 1

The selected square in the first screenshot is placed in the center of the Project's frame. You can read its coordinates on the x-axis ruler and y-axis ruler. Those coordinates are identical to the coordinates of the Shape's Control Points.

Screenshot 2

Now the upper square is selected and its coordinates in the Canvas are of course different. However, if you look at the coordinates in the Inspector, you can see that those coordinates are the same.

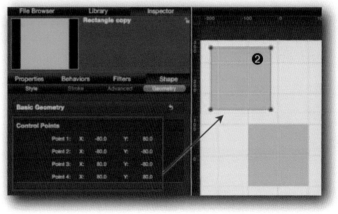

This shows that the Control Point coordinates in the Inspector have nothing to do with the actual placement in the Project, the coordinates in the Project frame. The Control Points are independent from the Project. The placement of the Object in the first screenshot is just the exception when the Object is centered at the 0/0 coordinate in the Project.

➡ Placing the Object

All the parameters that belong to this group will place the Object (the way it was "prepared") onto the Project frame.

There are three parameters that define the initial placement of the Object. These three parameters don't change the original shape (it's default Control Point coordinates), they only determine **where** and **how** to place the Object on the Project frame. The three parameters are Position, Anchor Point and Rotation.

☺ Position

The Position parameter has only the coordinates X, Y and Z (Z is only relevant in the 3D space). They represent the center point of an imaginary rectangle that is placed around the object so it touches the extreme point on the right, left, top and bottom of the Object. This way, it doesn't matter how asymmetrical or ill-shaped the object is, the surrounding frame is always a rectangle. The Position coordinates now place that Center point of the surrounding frame (and the Object inside it) at an absolute coordinate in the Project frame. That's why the coordinates of the Shape's Control Points have no relevance to the placement in the Project, only the Position parameter is responsible for that.

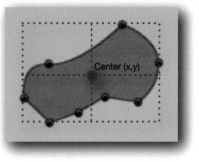

> Here is the simple formula (without the Anchor Point): Place the Center of the surrounding frame of an Object at the Position coordinates:

Center (x,y) = Position (x,y)

☺ Anchor Point

This parameter can be a little bit confusing because it includes two components.

> ▶ Rotational axis

The definition of the Anchor Point sounds fairly simple. It represents the axis that the Object can be rotated around. For example, take a piece of paper and pin it on the wall. When you stick the pin right in the center of the paper and spin the paper, it will rotate around its center axis. When you stick the pin at the lower right corner, then the paper will spin off center axis. The pin represents the axis and the Anchor Point represents that pin (That position is important later when you use the other parameter, Rotation).

That model however tells only half the story of what is happening with the Anchor Point in Motion. It explains the concept of the Anchor Point regarding the rotation. But there is a second component to it.

> ▶ Position offset

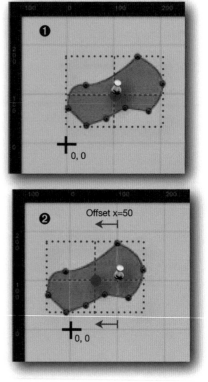

In the example, I assume that the paper is always at the same position on the wall and that I move the pin. But in Motion, it is the other way around. Imagine that you lift the pin (to keep it at the same position) and now you move the paper underneath it. And this is the second component of the Anchor Point. It actually moves the position of the Object ("moving the paper underneath") by the Anchor Point value.

While the coordinates of the Position represent an absolute position in the Project frame, the coordinates for the Anchor Point represent a relative position, an offset value. It is the distance that the center point of the surrounding frame of the Object moves away from the Position coordinates.

The first diagram ❶ shows an Object in the Canvas with the Position value of x=100, y=100 (blue circle). The Anchor Point (pin) value is zero. This means that the Position value defines the Center of the Object AND the Anchor Point.

In the second diagram ❷, the Anchor Point value is x=50, y=0. The coordinates for the Anchor Point (pin) are still defined by the coordinates of the Position. However, the Anchor value shifts the Center point of the Object (blue circle) exactly by the value of the Anchor Point.

Here are the two formulas:

The rotation axis of the Object is always defined by the Position coordinates

Anchor (x,y) = Position (x,y)

The actual placement (x,y) of the Object, its center point, is the Position value minus the Anchor Point value.

Center (x,y) = Position (x,y) - Anchor (x,y)

💡 Rotation

The Rotation value defines the angle, to what degree the object is rotated around its axis. Please be aware of the following facts:

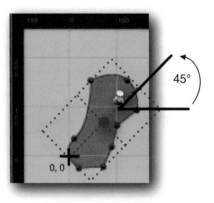

- The rotation doesn't change the shape of the Object (if looked directly at it).
- You can rotate around any of the three axes: x, y and z.
- All the axes cross the coordinate of the Anchor Point that is identical to the Position coordinates.
- You can set an angle greater than 360°. This wouldn't make much sense for a still image but i.e. when you animate the Rotation, a value of 1080° means to fully rotate the Object 3 times.

Parameters in the Inspector

All three parameters responsible for placing the Object are located in the Transform module of the Inspector's Properties tab. Position and Anchor Points display the X and Y coordinates and the Rotation displays the angle for the Z-axis. Expanding the view will display all three axes for those parameters.

And don't forget to use the Reset Button or Reset command to quickly place the Object in the center of the Project frame (x=0, y=0)

Parameters in the Canvas

The three parameters are also visible and adjustable in the Canvas via onscreen controls. However, pay attention to the subtle differences regarding what Tool is selected.

- Drag the Rotation Handle with the Object: Transform and 3D Transform Tool
- Drag the Rotation Handle without the Object: Anchor Point Tool. This also changes the Position value by the same amount.
- Moving the Object always drags the Rotation Handle with it.
- Rotate the Object: The Transform tool rotates only around the z-axis where the 3D Transform tool can rotate around all three axes. The Anchor Point tool cannot rotate at all.

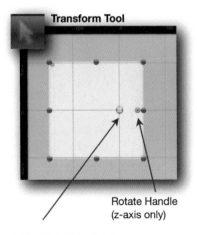

Transform Tool

Rotate Handle
(z-axis only)

Moves Anchor Point
with Object in x/y field
(drag Anchor handle)

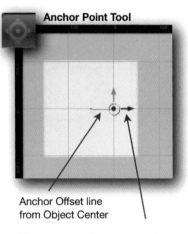

Anchor Point Tool

Anchor Offset line
from Object Center

Moves Anchor Point without Object
on x, y or z axis (drag arrows). Also
moves the Position value

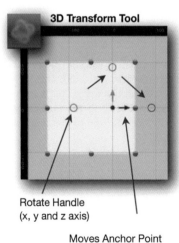

3D Transform Tool

Rotate Handle
(x, y and z axis)

Moves Anchor Point
with Object on x, y or
z axis (drag arrows)

➡ Altering the Object

The third group of parameters are the ones that can alter the existing Object. Of course there are a multitude of parameters that can change an Object but I'm concentrating on the main parameters that alter its original shape, appearance and placement. Those parameters are Transform, Distort and Crop located under the Properties tab.

💡 Transform

The Transform module includes a total of five different parameters. I included three of them in the previous group about "Placing the Object". I put the other two parameters Scale and Shear here in the "Altering the Object" group because they can alter the original shape and position of the Object.

▶ Scale

This parameter provides four sliders in the Inspector. A master slider (Compound Parameter) that alters all three axes proportionally and if you expand the parameter you can adjust each of the three axis separately (Sub-Parameters). Changing all the values at the same time increases or decreases the size of the Object while maintaining its shape. Changing individual sliders will alter the shape of the Object.

Pay attention to the Control Points. They move along with the altered shape but when you check the Control Point coordinates in the Geometry tab, you will see that they stayed the same. So the changes are not applied directly to the original Object (its Control Points), but applied as an offset value.

▶ Shear

The Shear effect makes a parallelogram out of a rectangle by shifting the two parallel sides away from each other, parallel to the x-axis or y-axis. The rectangle in this case is not the shape of the Object but the surrounding frame that I talked about earlier when we positioned the Object.

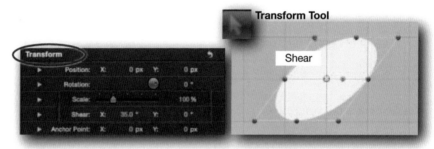

▶ Transform Handles (Position+Scale):

This is not another parameter in the Inspector. These are the onscreen controls in the Canvas when the Transform tool is selected. Those eight handles (four corners, four sides) can push and pull on the surrounding frame, transforming the Object inside. This effectively alters the Position and Scale value at the same time depending on how you drag the handles.

On an Object with visible Control Points, you can drag an area around it and select the command "*Transform Control Points*" from the Edit Menu (Key Command sh+cmd+T). This creates a white rectangle *Transform Box* with transform handles so its sides cross the outer most Control Points of the selected area. Adjusting any Transform parameters, now affects only the Control Points inside that box.

💡 Distort

Unfortunately, Motion uses again two different terms for the same thing. The tool in the Canvas is called "Distort" but the module in the Inspector's Properties tab is called "Four Corner".

The parameter lets you reposition any of the four corners of the surrounding frame (x/y coordinates) while keeping the other three corners in place. This results in a geometrical distortion of the shape.

💡 Crop

This is the standard crop effect which functions as a mask that you can pull over from any of the four sides. The Inspector lets you adjust one side at a time with the sliders. The eight handles of the Crop tool in the Canvas lets you adjust two sides at a time when you drag a corner handle. You can also drag the Object which will slide the underlying Object against the mask.

Please note that you have to disable the Distort module to make proper Crop adjustments.

Text

Text is an important part of Motion and motion graphics application in general. In addition to creating great looking text, you can animate that text and treat it with the same cool effects as other Objects in Motion.

Toolbar

The procedure to enter text into your Project is very simple:

☑ Select the Text Tool from the Toolbar or use the Key Command **T** (the HUD won't display any tool properties for text).

☑ Click on the Canvas where you want to position the text.

- A blinking insert marker appears on the Canvas.
- A Text Object Layer will be created in the Layers List with the default name "Text".
- The Text Inspector and the HUD (if visible) display the default properties for the text object.

☑ (optional) Change the text properties in the HUD (or Inspector) to change the text format.

☑ Start to type the text. The Object name in the Layers List will change to whatever you type (until you overwrite the Object name in the Layers List).

☑ To finish the text, click the Text tool again or any other tool.

HUD (text)

▶ **Text Inspector**

The Text Object provides the most parameters of any object in Motion. You can tweak every imaginary aspect of how your text will look in your composition. Here is an overview of all the modules in the various Inspector tabs.

All four Inspector tabs are active:

◉ **Properties**: This tab includes the modules Transform, Blending and Timing which affect the Text Object as an Image Layer in the context of your composition.

◉ **Behavior**: Motion provides many text specific Behaviors that let you animate your text without any keyframing.

◉ **Filter**: Apply any filters to modify the look of your text even further.

◉ **Text**: This is the Object tab that lets you set the default attributes of your Text Object. The Text tab has all its modules grouped in three sub-tabs: Format - Style - Layout

It goes beyond the scope of this manual to cover all the text parameters. I just want to point out a few formatting aspects.

► **Basic Attributes**

The Basic Attributes include all the common parameters known from word processors (e.g. Font, Size, Alignments, Spacing etc.). They are listed under the Inspector ➤ Text ➤ Format ❶. The Collection and Font popup menus ❷ are the same as are listed in your standard OSX Fonts window. You will also find the same content under the Fonts category in the Library pane. The sidebar on the right ❸ lists the collections and the Stack below ❹ displays the available Fonts in the selected collection. When you scroll through the Fonts menu, the text in your Canvas will display them dynamically.

As I pointed out in the chapter about the Library, this is OSX content and Motion just displays it in the Library. Dragging a Font from the Library Stack onto a Text Object (in the Layers List or Canvas) has the same effect as selecting that font in the Inspector from the Font popup menu. Please note that you cannot move a text back to the Library's Fonts category (it is read only OSX content). You can move it to the Content, Favorites or Favorites Menu folder but this will create a copy of that Text Object and not just its font.

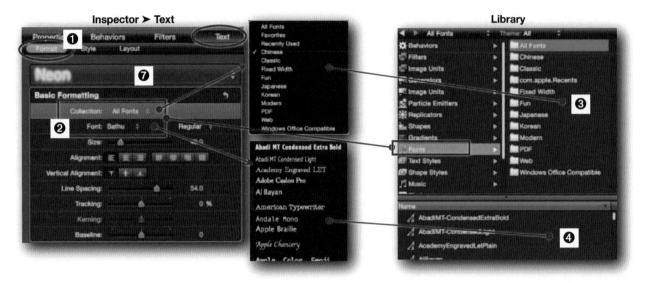

► **Style Attributes**

All the Attributes that go beyond the standard text formatting are grouped under the Style tab ❺. Motion provides 33 Text Styles that can be selected from this big popup menu ❻ at the top of the Inspector modules. This popup menu is also available in the Format tab ❼. It corresponds to the Text Styles category in the Library pane ❽.

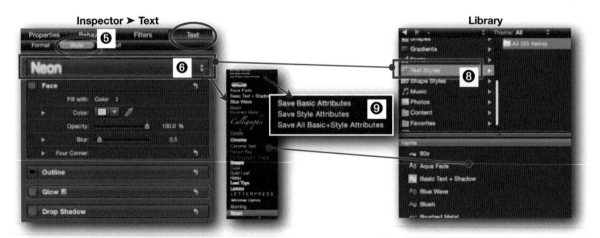

You can add your own Text Styles to the Text Styles category in the Library. However, you cannot drag the Text Object back to the Library because this saves the whole Text Object. Instead, use any of the three save commands at the top of the Styles Menu ❾. You can choose to save only the Basic, the Styles, or both Attributes as a new Text Styles. The custom Styles will be listed together with the factory styles in the styles popup menu in alphabetical order.

As standard procedure, the custom created Text Styles are stored as Motion Library Objects (.molo) to the Customs Library location *"username"/Library/ Application Support/ Motion/Library/Text Styles.*

9 - Effects

As with many tools and techniques nowadays, you can get some amazing results with just a few clicks in an app. However, if you want to get into more details and want to be in control beyond some popular presets, you have to understand the underlying concept. Motion's interface makes it really easy to accomplish even complex motion graphics effects. There are only a few basic concepts to understand first. In this chapter, I will introduce the various effects and tools with a focus on understanding those concepts. From then on, you can dive into the vast amount of available content in Motion and experiment with it.

Filter

Filters alter, change and mess around with an Object, whatever it is, an image, a video clip or an audio track. They are understood and used by everybody working in the graphics, video or audio fields. However, in Motion, the Filter effects only apply to Image Objects, not Audio Objects.

When altering Objects, always keep in mind **where** and **what** you are adjusting:

Internal Manipulation

This is the basic level where you change the properties (attributes, parameters, etc) of the Object itself. This happens "inside" the Object through the controllers for whatever properties are made available. No help, no external Filter Objects are needed for these adjustments "outside' the Object itself.

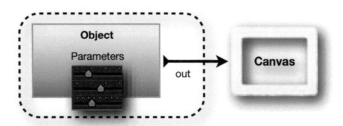

External Manipulation

A Filter in Motion is a set of additional effect parameters in the form of a plugin. It manipulates the Object from the "outside". This is an "external" manipulation compared to the Object's own "internal" manipulation parameters.

- The Filter is a separate Object that can be applied to an existing Image Object, even a Group Object.
- The Filter works as a Plug-in with its own set of parameters that can be edited in its own module.
- Think about an image in terms of a signal flow similar to an audio signal flow. The output of the Image Object "feeds" the input of the Filter Objects (the applied filter plugin) and its output is then visible on the Canvas (or is fed to the next Object in the Projects stacking order).
- Adding more than one Filter to an Object just adds more modules to that "chain" in the signal flow. The order of the sequence might be important depending on the used Filter.

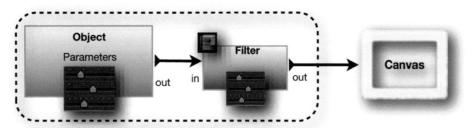

▶ About Filters

- As a Plug-in, a Filter cannot exist by itself. It has to be "attached" to an Image Object.
- Filters can only be applied to Image Layers from inside of Motion, from the Motion Library to be specific.
- Filters are small files called "Motion Library Objects" (.molo) that have to be stored in any of two folder locations on your drive (Factory or Custom location) so the Motion Library can display them.
- You can add your customized Filters that you use in your Motion Project back to the Library.
- You can access the available Filters from the Library pane or the Filter button on the Toolbar.

▶ Adding Filters

There are three ways to add a Filter:

- � Select an Image Object first and apply the Filter Object to it.
- 💷 Select a Filter from the Toolbar button menu
- 💷 Drag the Filter Object directly onto the Image Object in any of the windows (Project Pane, Timing Pane or Canvas).

▶ Rearrange Filter

Filter Objects behave like any other Objects so all the standard operations and Key Commands apply.

- 💷 **Drag:** You can drag the Filter Object to many places to change the order inside a Layer: Drag the modules inside the Inspector's Filter tab ❶ or drag the Filter Object in the Layers List ❷ (Project Pane or Timing Pane). In the Layers List, you can even drag a Filter to a different Layer. Dragging the Filter Object on the Timeline ❸ lets you adjust its timing position.

- 💷 **Command**: Select any Filter Object(s) and choose a command from the Edit Menu (cut, copy, paste, duplicate) or use their Key Commands.

Toolbar

Library Pane

Preview Filter

▶ Adjust Filter

Use the bypass button ❹ on the Inspector module or the checkbox ❺ in the Layers List to bypass the Filter for quick AB comparison when you adjust the Filter.

- 💡 **Inspector** (Filter Tab): Filters don't have their own Inspector Objects like Shapes, Text, etc. They become part of the Image Layer they are attached to. All the Filters that are assigned to a specific Object are visible under the Inspector's Filter Tab for that Object ❶.

- 💡 **HUD**: Once a Filter is applied to an Object, its main Parameters are also available in the HUD. Select them from the popup menu ❻ on the HUD's header.

- 💡 **Canvas**: Some Filter parameters are available as onscreen controls ❼.

- 💡 **Keyframes/Behaviors:** You can automate Filter parameters over time with Keyframes or Behavior simulations.

▶ Remove Filter

- 💷 Delete the selected Object(s) from the Layers List or the Timeline
- 💷 Delete the selected Filter module from the Filters Tab of the Objects Inspector.

▶ And also

- The Filter Clips in the Timeline are purple ❸.
- You can lock Filters ❷ the same way as other Objects in the Layers List to avoid accidental changes.
- Disabled Filter Objects are grayed out ❷.
- The preview section at the top of the Library simulates the effect in that thumbnail (that simulation is not available for the Image Units).
- You can disable all Filters for an Object in the Layers List by clicking on the Filters Icon ❷ next to the Object: ⬛ enabled, ⬛ disabled.

Layers List

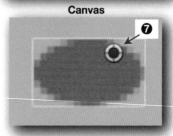

Timeline

Canvas

Inspector ➤ Filter tab

HUD

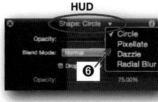

Behavior

Behaviors are another type of Effect Object. They differ from a static Filter effect in that Behaviors are *motion* effects. Like filters, they function as Plug-ins that can be assigned to a wide variety of Objects.

Behaviors are motion effects.

I already covered Keyframes which is another tool that lets you create motion effects (change or animate parameters over time). But there are differences between Keyframes and Behaviors.

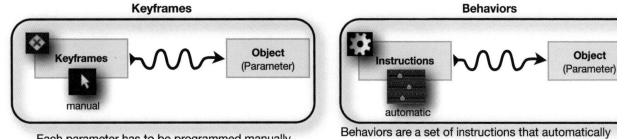

Each parameter has to be programmed manually by creating Keyframes to get the resulting animation curve for the motion effect.

Behaviors are a set of instructions that automatically manipulate the parameter(s) of the target Object. Instead of editing the parameters of the Object, you edit the parameters of the Behavior's instructions set.

With Keyframes, you have to know exactly which parameter to animate in order to get a specific motion effect. With Behaviors you don't. You can create complex motion effects that would be very hard or close to impossible to do with Keyframes, i.e. simulation of physical behaviors and interaction with other Objects in the Composition.

Types of Behaviors

Motion provides a huge collection of Behaviors in its Library. Although they are organized in categories, it is not really clear that there are two main types of Behaviors. I extended the diagram I used in the previous Filter section to show the functionality of those two Behavior types: **Object Behaviors** and **Parameter Behaviors**. They have a slightly different icon in the Layers List. Please keep in mind that this is a very simplified model and some Behaviors are more complex.

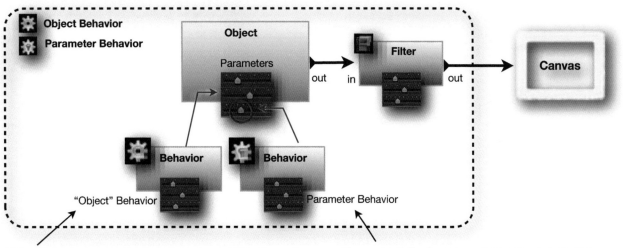

Object Behaviors are designated for one type of Object e.g., shape, text, audio, etc. They provide motion effects that affect the parameters of the Object. You don't have to know what the parameters are because the Behavior makes it easy by providing simple controls to change its behavior. These can be simple parameter controls (e.g., faster, slower, bigger, more-less) or visual onscreen controls.

Parameter Behavior are small instruction sets that let you generate values i.e. based on mathematical functions like oscillate, randomize. Those instructions are then applied (via a popup menu) to a single Parameter of the current Object.

As with the Filter Objects, you can access the available Behaviors from the Library Pane or the Behaviors button on the Toolbar. The different categories are organized in folders that represent the different types of Behavior. The names of the folders indicate the type of Behaviors they include (Audio, Camera, Shape, Text, etc). Please note that you cannot apply a Behaviors Object to an Object that it is not intended for, i.e. apply Shape behaviors to a Text Object.

The list of folders in the Library doesn't emphasize the two different types of Behaviors. The Parameter Behaviors are grouped in just another folder, the "Parameter" folder, next to all the other (non-Parameter) Object Behaviors folders.

In general, managing Behavior Objects is very similar to managing Filter Objects.

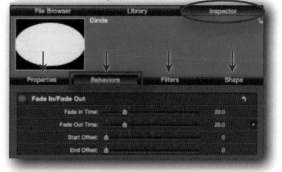

▶ **About Behaviors**

- As a Plug-in, a Behavior cannot exist by itself. It has to be "attached" to another Object.

- Behaviors can only be applied to Objects from inside of Motion, from the Motion Library to be specific.

- Behaviors are small files called "Motion Library Objects" (.molo) that have to be stored in any of two folder locations on your drive (Factory or Custom location) so the Motion Library can display them.

- You can add your custom Behavior in Motion from your Project back to the Library.

Now the four tabs in the Inspector are complete:

- ☑ **Properties** Tab: Includes all the modules that define the Object in the Project.

- ☑ **Behaviors** Tab: Includes all the Behavior plugins that are assigned to this Object.

- ☑ **Filters** Tab: Includes all the Filter plugins that are assigned to this Object.

- ☑ **"Object"** Tab (name after the Objet type): Includes all the modules that define the basic attributes of the Object.

▶ **Adding Behaviors**

There are two ways to add a Behavior. Remember that Behavior Objects are "Object aware". Objects can only be applied to Objects they are intended for.

- Select an Object first and apply the Behavior Object to it. Click the Apply button in the Library.

- Select a Behavior from the Toolbar button menu.

- Drag the Behavior Object directly onto the Object in any of the windows (Project Pane, Timing Pane or Canvas).

When controlled by a Behavior, the Parameter in the Inspector displays a little gear icon where it would usually displays the diamond shaped Keyframe icon. This indicates that the Parameter is controlled by a Behavior. If that Parameter is controlled by a Behavior and Keyframes, then those Keyframe diamonds have an additional little gear icon inside.

Inspector

Blending	
Opacity: 100.0 % ⚙	

Behaviors only   Keyframes only   Behaviors and Keyframes   Behaviors and Keyframes (Keyframe selected)

▸ **Rearrange Behavior**

Behavior Objects act like any other Objects so all the standard operations and Key Commands apply.

> **Drag:** You can drag the Behavior Object in many places to change the order inside a Layer: Drag the modules inside the Inspector's Behavior tab ❶ or drag the Behavior Object in the Layers List ❷ (Project Pane of Timing Pane). In the Layers List, you can even drag a Behavior to a different Layer. Dragging the Behavior Object on the Timeline ❸ lets you adjust its timing position.

> **Command**: Select any Behavior Object(s) and choose a commands from the Edit Menu (cut, copy, paste, duplicate) or use their Key Commands.

▸ **Adjust Behavior**

Use the bypass button ❹ on the Inspector module or the checkbox ❺ in the Layers List to bypass the Behavior for quick AB comparison when you adjust the Behavior.

> **Inspector** (Behavior Tab): Behaviors don't have their own Inspector Objects like Shapes, Text, etc. They become part of the Object they are attached to. All the Behaviors that are assigned to a specific Object are visible under the Inspector's Behavior Tab for that Object ❶.

> **HUD**: Once a Behavior is applied to an Object, its main Parameters are also available in the HUD. Select them from the popup menu ❻ on the HUD's header.

> **Canvas**: Some Behavior parameters are available as onscreen controls ❼.

▸ **Remove Behavior**

> Delete the selected Object(s) from the Layers List or the Timeline.

> Delete the selected Behavior module from the Behavior Tab of the Objects Inspector.

▸ **And also**

- The Behavior Clips in the Timeline are also purple ❸ like the Filters.

- You can lock Behaviors ❷ in the same way as other Objects in the Layers List to avoid accidental changes.

- Disabled Behavior Objects are grayed out ❷

- Preview section at the top of the Library simulates the effect in that thumbnail.

- You can disable all Behaviors for an Object in the Layers List by clicking on the Behaviors Icon ❷ next to the Object:

  enabled, disabled

▸ **Convert Behaviors to Keyframes**

Most of the Behaviors modify existing Parameters of its target Object over time. This is the same principle as with Keyframe animation and that's why the animation curve caused by a Behavior is also displayed in the Keyframe Timeline. It is a solid line (curve) without any Keyframes.

You can Convert that Behavior Animation to Keyframes if you want to tweak it manually. Select from the Main Menu Object ➤ Convert To Keyframes ... or use the Key Command cmd+K. An Alert window will warn you that only dedicated parameter values can be converted to Keyframes, not any interactive motion with other Objects. Please note that the Behavior Object will be deleted after the conversion.

Layers List

Timeline

Canvas

Inspector ➤ Behaviors tab

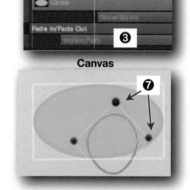

HUD

Keyframe Timeline with Behavior Curve   convert   **Keyframe Timeline with Keyframe Curve**

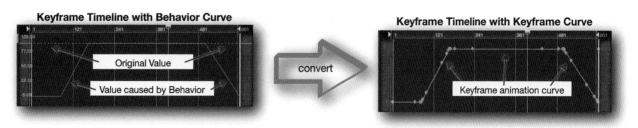

Original Value

Value caused by Behavior

Keyframe animation curve

Particle System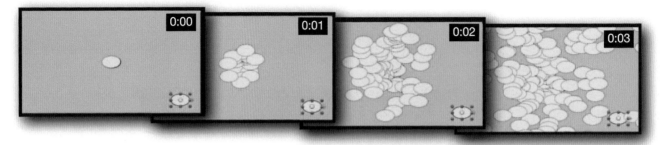

The "Particle System" in Motion is an effect for creating dynamic simulations. It is a very sophisticated type of effect that lets you create large numbers of Objects that are animated (change over time), spread out from one location (emitted) and "live" only for a specified amount of time (expire).

Here is a simple example of a Particle System that is emitting Particles over the duration of 3 seconds.

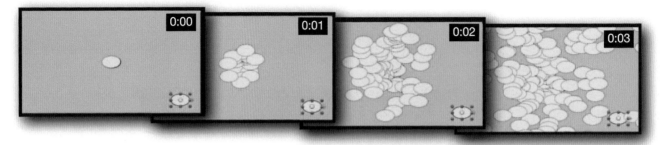

A Particle System is called a system because, unlike Filters or Behaviors that are single component, the Particle System is made of several components in order to create such an effect.

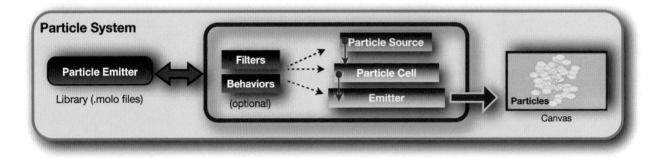

Particle System

This is the name that describes the whole concept with all the components needed to setup a Particle System.

Particle Source

At the very beginning, a Particle System needs an Image Layer in the Layers List as its source. This is also called the Source Object, the visual material the effect is based on. Without it, the Particle System has no visual output.

- The Particle Source can be positioned anywhere in the Layers List. The place of that Object has no effect on the Particle System.
- The Particle Source can even be deactivated (and most likely it is) because it is used as source material and not necessarily as a visual element on its own in your Composition.
- Any modification to the Particle Source affects the Particle System because it is linked to that Image Layer.

Particle Cell

The next level is the Particle Cell, or just the Cell. It determines the look of the single particles in a Particle System. A single Particle Source (Image Layer) has to be assigned to a Cell, it inherits the look of that Image Layer. This establishes an "active" link between the Source Object and the Cell. Modifying the Source Object changes the Cell.

The Cell parameters now let you further manipulate the visual appearance of the Source Object. Please note that this doesn't change the Source Object, it's more like an added filter layer.

Emitter

The Emitter sets the rules about how to turn the Cell into Particles that spread out on the Canvas. Its parameters let you manipulate the overall movement (animation) of those emerging particles.

Particles

The Particles are the resulting objects on the Canvas that are generated by the Emitter.

Particle Emitter (preset)

This is the preset, available from the Motion Library, that includes all the components for a specific Particle System effect.

One Particle System consists of a single Emitter. However, the Emitter itself can have multiple Cells and those Cells can be linked to the same Source Object (Image Layer) or a different Source Object.

Here is an example for three different setups for Emitters:

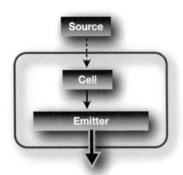

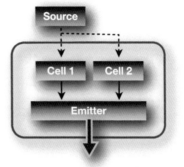

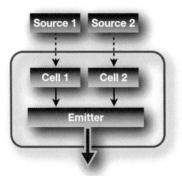

The Emitter contains only one Cell that is assigned to a Source.

The Emitter contains two Cells that have the same Source assigned to them.

The Emitter contains two Cells, each assigned to its own Source.

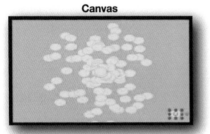

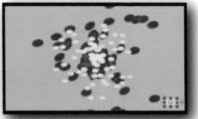

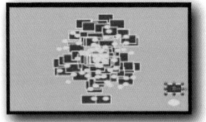

The Emitter effect is based on only one type of Image Layer. The selected Image in the lower right corner is the active (visible) Source Object.

Both Cells have the same Source Object (Circe) but the individual Cell parameters are different (shape, color, etc)

Both Cells have different Image Layers as their source (circle, rectangle).

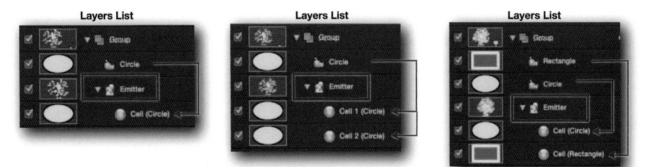

The Emitter is the main Image Layer of the Particle System. Its Cell(s) are included "inside" as sublayers below the Emitter. You can enable/disable individual Cells or switch the whole Particle System by unchecking the Emitter checkbox.
In this example, I left the Image Layer, that is used as the Source Object, active so you can see it in the lower right corner of the Canvas screenshot. Usually that Image Layer is inactive because it is only used as source material and not as a visual element on its own as part of your composition.

These are three examples of a basic setup. You can extend the elements even further for more complex Particle Systems. In addition, each of those three elements can have **Masks** (Source), **Filters** (Source, Emitter) and **Behavior** (Source, Cell, Emitter). At that level, the possibilities are limitless.

Editing Particle Systems

Select either the Emitter or the Cell to access their parameters in the Inspector.

▸ **Particle Cell**

The Object tab in the Inspector is labeled "Particle Cell" ❶. It includes only one module, the *Cell Controls* with all the parameters that define how the Particles look and behave. At the bottom is the assignment for the Particle Source ❷. This is an Object Well where you can drag an Image Layer from the Layers List onto it to reassign the Particle Source.

The Properties tab contains only the Timing module. The Filter tab is not available (grayed out), however the Behaviors tab is active ❸. This means you can apply Behavior animation in addition to the motion that is defined in the Particle system.

▸ **Emitter**

The Object tab in the Inspector is labeled "Emitter" ❹. This tab has a specialty. It includes the modules for the *Emitter Controls* and the *Cell Controls* ❺ so, as a convenience, you don't have to switch the Inspector view.

However, if the Emitter has more than one Cell, then instead of the Cell Controls, the window displays a *Master Controls* module ❻ that affects all the Cells (in percentage). A third module, *Cells* ❼, lists all the Cells for that Emitter. Here you can enable/disable individual Cells and reassign new Particle Sources by dragging Image Layers onto their Source Well.

The Properties tab includes most of the transform modules for a standard layer to adjust the basic shape and position of the Emitter as a whole. The Emitter also has the option to assign Behaviors and Filters ❽ to it, extending the level of manipulation even further.

Keyframes

Most of the Parameters can be animated with Keyframes for even more flexibility.

HUD

Both, Particle Cells and Emitter also provide a subset of their parameters in the HUD. The Emitter even has visual controls for 2D and 3D depending on the settings ❾.

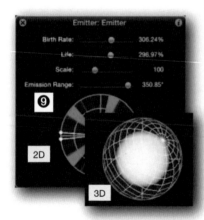

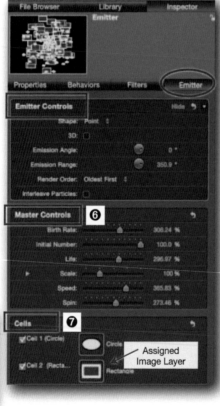

Create Particle Systems

There are two ways to create Particle Systems. You can create a new one based on an Image Layer in your current Project (that will become the Particle Source) or use any of the hundreds of ready to use Particle Emitters from the Library.

► Create new Particle System

☑ Select an Image Layer in your Project's Layers List that you want to use as the Particle Source in your Particle System. The position of that Layer (in the Canvas and Layers List) will be the initial position for the Emitter Object. You can even use a whole Group Layer as the Source Object. The more complex the Source Object is (video with applied filters or complex groups), the more demanding the Emitter will be on the computer's CPU when it has to render all those motion effects in real time.

☑ Use any of the three commands to create the Particle System:

Toolbar

- 💡 Click on the Particle System button on the right side of the Toolbar
- 💡 Main Menu Command Object ➤ Make Particle
- 💡 Key Command E

☑ The following things will happen:

- The selected Image Layer (Particle Source) will be deselected.
- A new Emitter Layer will be created above that Image Layer.
- A Particle Cell Layer will be create as a sublayer below the Emitter Layer. The Cell inherits its name from the Particle Source.

► Use existing Particle System

The Library provides over 200 Particle Systems. They are available as objects called *Particle Emitters*. These are "self-contained" presets that include all the elements including the Particle Source. Many of the presets have assigned Behaviors for the Emitter and/or the Cell.

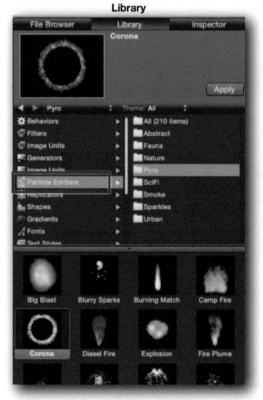

☑ Open the Library and select "Particle Emitters" from the left column in the sidebar.

☑ The right column of the Sidebar contains the various presets organized in theme folders. Select a folder to display its content in the Stack below (use Icon View in the Stack to see a picture of the effect).

☑ Click on a Particle Emitter preset in the Stack to preview a simulation of the resulting effect in the Preview thumbnail at the top of the Library window.

☑ Drag the preset from the Stack onto any of your Project window panes (Layers List, Timeline, Canvas) or click the "Apply" button in the Preview section.

► Save Particle Emitter Presets

As with other effect objects, you can save (customized) Particle Systems from your Project back to the Library for use in other Projects. Just drag the Emitter Layer to the Content, Favorites, Favorites Menu or the Particle Emitters folder in the Library. Motion will create a Particle Emitter preset in that folder which is a representation of a .molo file that is created in your custom location. *"username"/Library/Application Support/Motion/Library/*.

All the other elements of the Particle System (Cell, Particle Source, Behaviors, Filters) will be included in that preset.

Replicator Pattern

The Replicator in Motion is an effect that builds pattern of repeating elements based on an existing image layer (video, graphics, shape, text). Unlike the Particle System that emits dynamic objects that change over time and disappear, a Replicator generates static objects to build its pattern. However those objects can be animated with Behaviors and Keyframes.

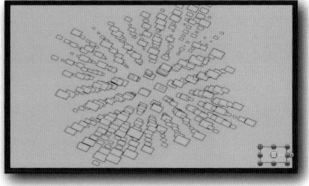

Here is a simple example of a Replicator Pattern created out of a single green rectangle. The Source Object is the selected green rectangle in the lower right corner.

Similar to the Particle System, the Replicator Pattern is based on several components.

💡 Replicator Pattern

Instead of just Replicator, I prefer the term Replicator Pattern for the whole system with all its components.

💡 Object Source

As with the Particle System, a Replicator Pattern needs an Image Layer in the Layers List as its source. This is called the *Object Source*, the visual material the effect is based on. Without it, the Replicator Pattern has no visual output.

- The Object Source can be positioned anywhere in the Layers List. The place of that Object has no effect on the Replicator Pattern.
- The Object Source can even be deactivated (and most likely it is) because it is used as source material and not necessarily as a visual element on its own in your composition.
- Any modification to the (disabled) Image Layer that is used as the Object Source affects the Replicator Pattern because it is linked to that Image Layer.

💡 Replicator Cell

The next level is the Replicator Cell, or just the Cell. It determines the look of the single elements that form the pattern. A single Source Object (Image Layer) has to be assigned to a Cell which inherits the look of that Image Layer. This establishes an "active" link between the Object Source and the Cell. Modifying the Object Source changes the Cell.

The Cell parameters now let you further manipulate the visual appearance of the Object Source. Please note that this doesn't change the Object Source, it's more like an added filter layer.

💡 Replicator

The Replicator sets the rules of how the onscreen pattern will look, the various geometric shapes.

💡 Pattern (of elements)

The Pattern, made of single elements based on the Cell, is the final creation of the Replicator that appears in the Canvas.

💡 Replicator (preset)

This is the preset, available from the Motion Library, that includes all the components for a specific Replicator Pattern.

One Replicator Pattern consists of a single Replicator. However, the Replicator itself can have multiple Cells and those Cells can be linked to the same Object Source (Image Layer) or different Object Sources.

Here is an example for three different setups for a Replicator:

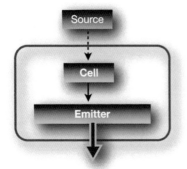

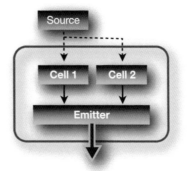

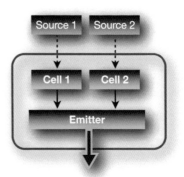

The Replicator contains only one Cell that is assigned to a Source.

The Replicator contains two Cells that have the same Source assigned to it.

The Replicator contains two Cells, each assigned to its own Source.

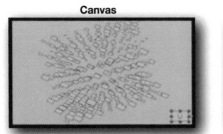

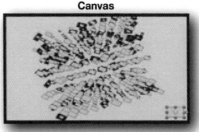

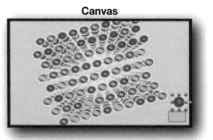

The Replicator Pattern is based on only one Image Layer. The selected Image in the lower right corner is the active (visible) Object Source.

Both Cells have the same Object Source but the individual Cell parameters are different (shape, color, etc)

Both Cells have different Image Layers as their source (circle, rectangle).

The Replicator is the main Image Layer for a Replicator Pattern. Its Cell(s) are included "inside" as sublayers below the Replicator. You can enable/disable individual Cells or switch the whole Replicator Pattern by unchecking the Replicator checkbox.
In this example, I left the Image Layer, that is used as the Source Object, active so you can see it in the lower right corner of the Canvas screenshot. Usually that Image Layer is inactive because it is only used as source material and not as a visual element on its own as part of your composition.

As with the general stacking order of Image Layers in the Layers List (*Layer Order*), the stacking order of multiple Cells inside a Replicator is also important for the appearance of the Pattern.

You can extend the elements even further for more complex Replicator Patterns. In addition, each of those three components can have **Masks** (Source), **Filters** (Source, Replicator) and **Behavior** (Source, Cell, Replicator). At that level, the possibilities are limitless.

Editing Replicator Patterns

Select either the Replicator or the Cell to access their parameters in the Inspector.

▶ Replicator Cell

The Object tab in the Inspector is labeled "Replicator Cell" **❶**. It includes only one module, the *Cell Controls* with all the parameters that define how the elements in a Pattern look and behave. At the bottom is the assignment for the Object Source. This is a Source Well where you can drag an Image Layer from the Layers List to reassign an Image Layer as the Object Source **❷**.

The Properties tab contains only the Timing module. The Filter tab is not available (grayed out), however the Behaviors tab is active **❸**. This means you can apply Behavior animation to the otherwise static Replicator Pattern.

▶ Replicator

The Object tab in the Inspector is labeled "Replicator" **❹**. This tab has a specialty. It includes the modules for the *Replicator Controls* and the *Cell Controls* **❺** so, as a convenience, you don't have to switch the Inspector view.

However, if the Replicator has more than one Cell, then instead of the Cell Controls, the window displays the *Replicator Controls* module and the *Cells* module **❼** which lists all the Cells for that Replicator. Here you can enable/disable individual Cells and reassign new Object Sources by dragging Image Layers onto their Source Well.

The parameters in the Replicator Controls module determine the shape and structure of the Pattern. The available parameters vary depending on the selection of the Shape popup menu **❻**. It provides different shapes including "Image". This selection adds another Source Well where you can drag any Image Layer and the Pattern will adopt its shape. *Box* and *Shape* are best suited for 3D Patterns.

The Properties tab includes the Transform, Blending and Timing module. The Behaviors and Filters tabs **❽** are available to extend the level of manipulation even further.

Keyframes

Most of the parameters can be animated with Keyframes to change the patterns dynamically.

HUD

Both, Particle Cells and Replicator also provide a subset of their parameters in the HUD **❾**.

Create Replicator Pattern

There are two ways to create Replicator Patterns. You can create a new one based on an Image Layer in your current Project (that will become the Object Source) or use any of the hundreds of ready to use Replicator Patterns from the Library.

▶ **Create new Replicator Pattern**

☑ Select an Image Layer in your Project's Layers List that you want to use as the Object Source in your Replicator Pattern. The position of that Layer (in the Canvas and Layers List) will be the initial position for the Replicator Object. You can even use a whole Group Layer as the Object Source. The following objects can't be used as Object Source: Camera, Light, Rig, Emitter, and Replicator. The more complex the Object Source is (video with applied filters or complex groups), the more demanding the Emitter will be on the computer's CPU when it has to render all those motion effects in real time.

☑ Use any of the three commands to create the Replicator Pattern:

Toolbar

- Click on the Replicator button on the far right of the Toolbar
- Main Menu Command Object ➤ Replicate
- Key Command L

☑ The following things will happen:

- The selected Image Layer (Object Source) will be deselected.
- A new Replicator Layer will be created above that Image Layer.
- A Replicator Cell Layer will be create as a sublayer below the Replicator Layer. The Cell inherits its name from the Object Source.

▶ **Use existing Replicator Pattern**

The Library provides over 200 Replicator Patterns. They are available as Objects called Replicators. These are "self-contained" presets that include all the elements including the Object Source. Many of the presets have assigned Behaviors for the Replicators and/or the Cell.

Library

☑ Open the Library and select "Replicators" from the left column in the sidebar.

☑ The right column of the Sidebar contains the various presets organized in folders. Select a folder to display its content in the Stack below (use Icon View in the Stack to see a picture of the effect).

☑ Click on a Replicator preset in the Stack to preview a simulation of the resulting effect in the Preview thumbnail at the top of the Library window.

☑ Drag the preset from the Stack onto any of your Project window panes (Layers List, Timeline, Canvas) or click the "Apply" button in the Preview section.

▶ **Edit existing Replicator Pattern**

You can replace the Object Source of a Cell by simply dragging a new Image Layer in the Layers List over the Cell.

The Adjust Tool from the Toolbar lets you alter the shape of the pattern in the Canvas.

▶ **Save Replicator Pattern Presets**

As with other effect objects, you can save Replicator Patterns from your Project back to the Library for use in other Projects. Just drag the Replicator Layer to the Content, Favorites, Favorites Menu or the Replicator folder in the Library. Motion will create a Replicator Pattern preset in that folder which is a representation of a .molo file that is created in your custom location *"username"/Library/Application Support/Motion/Library/*.

All the other elements of the Replicator Pattern (Cell, Particle Source, Behaviors, Filters) will be included in that preset.

Rig

As with many components, when talking about Rigs, we can start with two basic questions: What is it and what is it used for?

What is a Rig

A Rig is like an Effects Rack. And like an Effects Rack which has only one main function ("house" a variety of effect modules), a Rig also has one main function: "house" Widgets, like a container.

In your Motion Project, a Rig is just another Object, a Controller Object, that you create in your Project. It is listed as its own Layer in the Layers List. The Widgets in a Rig also have to be create and configured. They are placed as sublayers below the Rig in the Layers List.

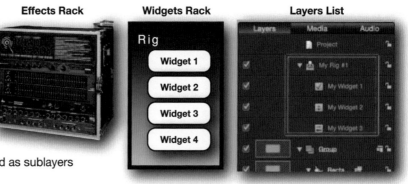

➡ Widgets

While a Rig is only the container that hosts the Widgets, the important parts are those Widgets which are little control modules that provide the actual controller functionality.

Before getting into the details about how to setup Widgets, let's try to understand the concept first.

The standard mechanism for editing parameter values of Objects in your Project is to select the Object that you want to edit first. Now the Inspector window and the HUD are automatically linked to that selected Object, displaying the values and controls for all the available parameters. In the Inspector, the parameters are grouped in window tabs and modules while the HUD displays only a subset of all the parameters. Adjusting the controls in any of the two windows will now affect the parameters for only that particular Object that is currently selected. Remember that the Inspector and HUD controls are identical, changing one will update the other and vice versa.

The Rig, with its containing Widgets however, is a Controller Object and that mechanism is quite different. Selecting a Rig will also link the Inspector and HUD to it, but this time, you don't want to edit the selected Rig (once it is configured). You use the custom configured controllers of the Widgets to edit parameters of Objects that are NOT currently selected. This is one specialty, a Widget can control any parameter of any Objects without having those Objects selected first.

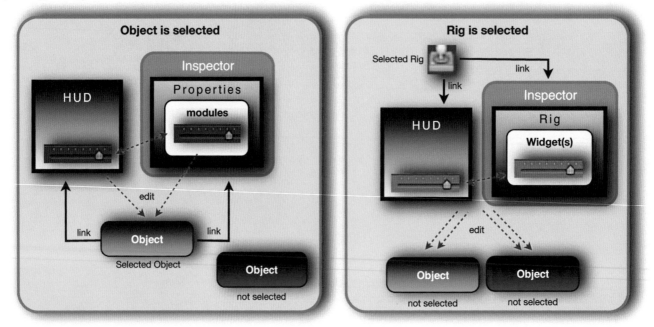

Of course you will also use the Inspector to configure and edit a selected Rig or Widget but the important difference is that you use the Rig and Widget Inspector to edit other, non-selected Objects with the Widget Controls.

Apple's documentation describes the Widgets as "master controls". However, I think that term might be misleading. Usually, a master controller is a separate parameter, a separate unit in a signal flow (i.e. channel fader vs master fader) but this is not the concept of a Widget.

Let's look at that in the context of the basic editing:

One Controller Window - One Parameter: An Object (shape, text, graphics, video, etc) is defined by its parameters. Motion, as any other application, provides controllers that let you manipulate those parameters. A controller window is linked to the window that displays the selected Object. Please note that this is a two way connection. The controller reads the current value of the parameter and when you change the controller, it writes (changes) the new value to that parameter.

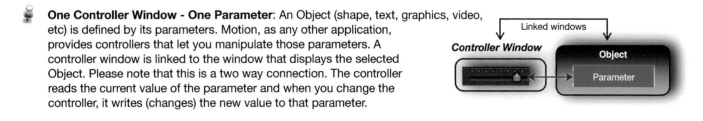

Many Controller Windows - One Parameter: The Controller window used in many applications is usually the Inspector. Motion however provides multiple windows. They have different advantages depending on what parameter you want to adjust. There are two things to pay attention to. All those controllers are virtually linked because they are connected to the same Parameters. Changing (write) the value in one controller window will update (read) the controller in the other windows. And again, the Inspector and its Mini-me, the HUD, are linked to the selected Object.

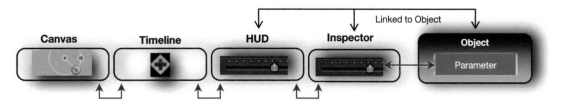

Many Controller Windows (including Widgets) - One Parameter: The Widget, which lets you configure custom controllers, is not just another controller window. It uses the Inspector and the HUD as its interface, by selecting a Widget. Remember, the Inspector and the HUD always display the parameters of the selected Object, in this case the Rig or Widget. The advantage is that the actual Object they are controlling, doesn't have to be selected.

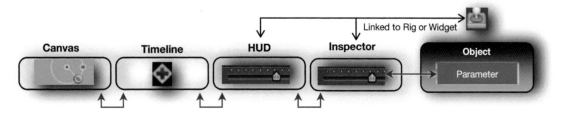

Many Controller Windows (including Widgets) - One Parameter (different Objects): Here you can see one advantage of Rigs. Every Widget inside a Rig can be configured to be the controller for a Parameter of a different Object (that don't have to be selected). This is really helpful when you have to make related adjustments to different Objects without the need to click between the Objects to switch the Inspector view.

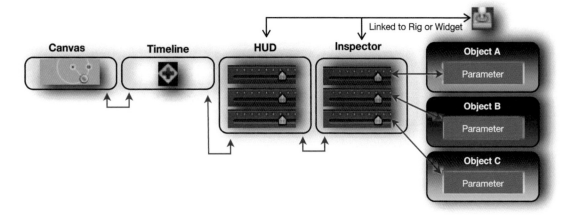

This was just a look at the relationship between the controller window and the Parameter that it is controlling. There is a second aspect of controllers that needs to be understood in the context of Widgets. That is the "master controller" or "macro controller".

One Controller - Many (related) Parameters: The real power of Widgets unfolds when controlling multiple Parameters with a single controller. This concept is already used with some of the parameters in the Inspector when adjusting a selected Object. These are the controllers with a disclosure triangle. They're called *Compound Parameter* because they don't represent a single Parameter but instead, a set of *Sub-Parameters*. For example, the Scale controller doesn't control a single "Scale" parameter. It controls three parameters which are its x,y and z coordinates. The Scale controller acts as a macro controller that is not connected to a single parameter, but steers the 3 controllers that are connected to the actual parameters (Scale X, Scale Y, Scale Y).

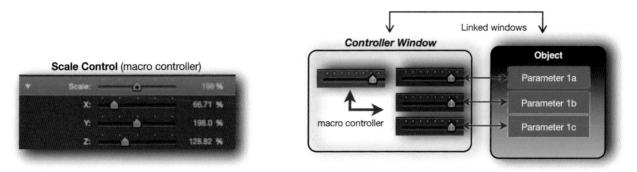

One Controller - Many (unrelated) Parameters: With Widgets, you can use the same concept of creating one controller that acts as a macro controller to steer other controls. But with Widgets, it is not restricted to the related coordinates of a parameter like we have seen with the Scale parameter. With Widgets, you can configure a macro controller that steers a selection on any controller available for an Object, even Parameters form different Objects. For example, a single slider could increase/decrease the Size, the Rotation and the Sheer of Object A and the Opacity of Object B, all at the same time in relationship to each other.

Now you understand two powerful features that are only possible with Rigs and Widgets but not possible with the standard editing tools in Motion: Controlling different <u>Objects</u> from one controller window and controlling different <u>Parameters</u> with one controller. Those extended functionalities are the main reason you would use Rigs and Widgets. They're even more important if you're customizing parameter controls for FCPx Templates to create a simple control interface for the Effect in FCPx.

What is a Rig used for

Edit multiple Objects from one Inspector window

Tweaking the parameters in different Objects (i.e. the opacity of Object A, B and C) requires that you select them one after another to bring up the Inspector or HUD to tweak those parameters. This requires a constant switching around between Objects. Instead, you create a RIG with three Widgets. One Widgets controls opacity of Object A, the second Widget controls the opacity of Object B and the third Widget controls Object C. Now, just select the Rig, which displays those three Widgets and its three controls, and you can adjust the opacity of all three Objects in one edit window.

Adjust multiple parameters simultaneously with a single controller

Often, if you have to change a specific parameter, another related parameter needs adjustment too. For example, if you want to change the thickness of the outline border of an Object when you increase the size of the Object, you assign both parameters to a single Widget Control.

Publish Widgets to a FCPx Template for easy adjustment of parameters

Whenever you save a Motion Project as a FCPx Template, you can choose specific parameters to become available for editing when opening the Motion Effect in FCPx. This process is called "publishing a parameter". In addition to publishing individual parameters, you can publish Widgets. With this in mind, you can configure Widgets that make it easy to adjust individual parameters or a complex set of parameters with a simple Widget control.

Create a Rig

There are three basic steps involved in creating a Rig:

- ☑ Create a Rig
- ☑ Create Widgets in that Rig
- ☑ Configure the Widgets

▶ **Create Rigs**

- 🧍 Use the Main Menu Command Object ➤ New Rig
- 🧍 Use the Key Command ctr+cmd+R
- 🧍 Use the command Add To Rig in the Inspector's Animation menu

▶ **Rules for Rigs**

- A new Rig, displayed as a Layer in the Layers List, will be placed on top of the List, below the Project Object ❶ .
- The Rig can be moved to any position in the Layers List. It is a Controller Object, not an Image Layer, and therefore has no effect on the stacking order.
- A Rig doesn't show up in the Canvas and although it is listed in the Timeline, it has only a black bar without a timing function.
- You can create as many Rigs as you want.
- You can (and should) rename Rigs and Widgets in the Layers List.

▶ **Properties**

The Rig has no properties by itself. Only the Object tab, labeled "Rig" ❷, is active in the Inspector. It contains two elements:

- 💡 Three buttons ❸ to create any of the three types of Widgets in this Rig.
- 💡 It displays all its Widgets as individual modules ❹ that let you configure them.

▶ **Add Widgets**

You create a new ("empty") Widget in the Rig with the Widget buttons or from a specific parameter in the Inspector's Animation menu. Once Widgets are created, you can move them freely between different Rigs if you want to organize them differently.

Create Widgets

A Widget is nothing other than a single control, available in the Inspector or the HUD. When you create a Widget, you basically create that single control, let's call it the "Widget Control". You can choose from three different types of controls, just click on any of the three buttons in the Rig Inspector to create one: a checkbox, a popup menu or a slider.

When you create a new Widget, it is "empty", without any functionality. Now you have to configure that Widget Control to decide what it should do.

Each new Widget will show up in the Layers List as a sublayer ❺

below the Rig and as a module ❹ in the Rig Inspector. The first thing you might want to do is to rename the Widget in the Layers List. This will be the name of the Widget Controller.

Rig: Add Widget buttons

You can view the Widget in its own Inspector view by selecting it in the Layers List. The Behaviors tab is active for animating the Widget.

Configure Widgets

Configuring a Widget means to setup the functionality of that single Widget Control (checkbox, popup menu or slider). In other words, what will happen later when you click that checkbox, select a menu item or move the slider.

The configuration of a Widget Control involves two components:

💡 **What parameter(s) does it control - Parameter Group**
As we have seen on the previous page, the power of Widgets lies in their flexibility. You can choose one or many of virtually any parameter from the available Objects in your Project (even another Widget) and control them as a group with that single Widget Control. So the first configuration step would be to choose the Parameter(s) from the available Objects. Those become the Target Parameters for the Widget Control. You can add new Parameters to that group (or remove them) at any time later.

> Please note that each parameter in your Project can be assigned to only one Widget! This is the reason why you can't duplicate or copy Rigs and Widgets.

💡 **What is the value of each parameter - Snapshot**
The other component of your Widget configuration is to match a specific position (state or value) of your Widget Controller to a specific value on the Target Parameters in its group. Remember, the Widget Control is not a one-to-one controller like an opacity slider in the Inspector and the HUD where moving one slider moves the other and vice versa. With Widgets, you have to define how the Widget Controller position translates into a specific value for each of the Target Parameters.

> For example, with a popup menu Widget Controller that has three menu items, each item represents a different value for the assigned Target Parameters.The Motion documentation calls this a Snapshot, which is a nice catchy term although a little bit misleading in my opinion. It is actually a "Value Set" which means "a list of all the Target Parameters and their specific values". The term Snapshot implies fixed values that have been set at a specific time. However, the value list here is dynamic which means you can change the items on that list (add/remove Target Parameters) and their values at any time.

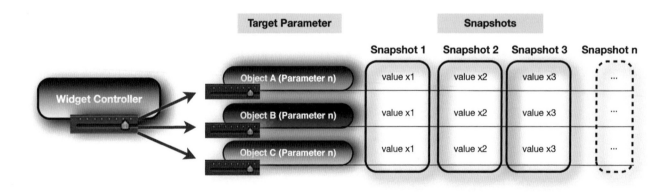

How a Widget Control works

It is important to understand that a Widget always stores discrete values for the Target Parameters. This makes sense for a controller that is a checkbox or a popup menu where you can switch between two or more states. But even with a slider control, the Widget relies on discrete values. You define two or more values on the slider (e.g., left, middle, right position) and the Widget then morphs between those values when you move the slider between those snapshot points. If you think about it, this is not a limitation but a powerful feature. For example you can limit the value range from minimum to maximum or influence the curve the way you position the discrete values across the slider.

As I mentioned before, when creating a new Widget, it will be "empty". It contains only the Widget Controller, no Target Parameter has been assigned yet. Now when you start configuring the Widgets, always keep the two components in mind:

💡 Adding a Target Parameter
💡 Setting the values for the Target Parameter

Add Parameters and Change Values

▶ **Adding Target Parameters**

There are three procedures for adding Target Parameters to a Widget:

Widget

📌 **Edit Mode**: This works much like recording Macro controllers (i.e. QuicKeys). On the Widget, click the "Start" button next to the Edit Mode. This activates the *snapshot recording mode*. You can now switch between Objects in your Project and when you adjust any parameter, that parameter of that specific Object will be added as a Target Parameter to the Widget with the value you just set. You can continue adding more parameters until you exit the recording mode by clicking the "Stop Rig Edit Mode" button on the floating window that is visible during the recording. (Click the X button in that window to abort the recording mode without any parameter assignment). You can use that method at any time to add more Target Parameters to a Widget.

📌 **Drag-and-Drop**: This procedure is even more intuitive. You just drag any Parameter Row from the Inspector window to the Widget's or Rig's Layers List.

Drop Menu

- Moving the Parameter Row over a Widget will add that Object's parameter as a Target Parameter to the Widget with its current value.

- Moving the Parameter Row over the Rig (or just above the first Widget) will assign that Parameter to a new Widget. If you release the mouse right away then it will be a slider Widget, if you wait a moment then a drop menu with three options appears. Select to add the dragged Parameter to a new slider, checkbox or popup menu.

📌 **Shortcut Menu:** On any Parameter in the Inspector, ctr+click to open its Shortcut Menu with the menu command Add to Rig. This opens up a submenu where you can select to which Rig/Widget you want to assign this parameter to. You can even assign it to a new Rig.

▶ **Changing values**

Here is a checkbox Widget in the Inspector that has three Target Parameters assigned to it. As you can see, the three Target Parameters have their original controls placed onto the Widget. These are exactly the same controls as in the Inspector and the HUD (if available). So the Widget, as a side effect, becomes another Edit Window for selected parameters, in addition to its original function as a complex macro controller.

Inspector ➤ Widget

Widget Type ◄
Widget Controller ◄
Adding Parameters ◄
Target Parameters ◄

This brings us back to the concept of Snapshots. Make sure you fully understand the following procedure or you might accidentally mess up your Project.

Once the first Target Parameter has been assigned to a Widget Controller, it will populate the available Snapshots (value lists) with the current value for that parameter. By default, the checkbox Widget controller has two Snapshots (checked/unchecked), the popup menu has three and the slider has one. However you can add more Snapshots to the popup menu and slider controller.

From now on, the Widget is always active (the blue bypass button in the Inspector and the checkbox in the Layers List have no effect!). It is important to take note of the currently selected Snapshot (the last menu item selection in the popup menu or the last state of the checkbox), or to remember what the last selected snapshot was before switching the Inspector view. This is called the "*Active Snapshot*". Think about the Widget (and its Active Snapshot) as another Edit Window like the Inspector or HUD.

Remember, if you change the opacity value for a parameter in the HUD to 50%, close the HUD, go to the Inspector, change that opacity value to 70% and go back and open the HUD, what you will see is the updated 70% value and not the 50% that you have "set" in the HUD. Because the HUD is just one of many controllers to the actual Parameter as I showed at the beginning of this section. Just think of the controllers for those Target Parameters in the Widget as part of another Edit Window that changes the parameter like the Inspector, the HUD or even the onscreen controls in the Canvas. Now you might understand why I have a problem with the term "Snapshot". It makes sense for "taking a snapshot" of the initial values, but those values are just a list that can be overwritten by the Target Parameter controls in the Widget or any other edit window controller if that snapshot is the current Active Snapshot (was last selected in the Widget). So the values of the Active Snapshot can always be changed by controls in other edit windows.

There is one exception: If a Parameter is assigned to a slider Widget Controller, then that parameter cannot be edited in other edit window anymore! It is "locked" by the Widget.

- **Adding Snapshots**

Here are the three Widget types with their interface elements:

Checkbox

A checkbox has two Snapshots (value sets), one for the checked and one for the unchecked state. You switch between them with the checkmark.

Popup menu

The default Widget has three menu items but you can add or remove item with the plus and minus button next to it. Renaming them is also a good idea. You can switch between the value sets by selecting them from the menu. The Options section lets you configure the menu behavior.

Slider

The slider is a more complex Widget. I explained earlier that although it is a continuos controller, its functionality is based on discrete values (snapshots). The Widget then interpolate between those values when you move the slider. Those discrete snapshots are represented by the little dots, the *tags,* below the slider.

Click on a tag to select its snapshot values (turns blue). Double+click below the slider to create a new snapshot, drag them left or right (change order) or all the way to the left to remove them with a "puff of smoke". The Option section provides further configuration controls.

Slider Widget controllers can be animated with Keyframes.

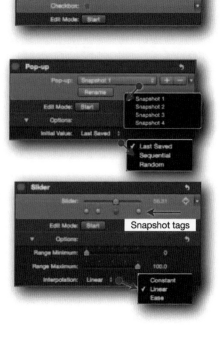

Those three screenshots of the Widget don't include any Target Parameters. But remember, when adding Target Parameters to those Widgets, whatever Snapshot you select last becomes the Active Snapshot and its values represent the current editing state which can be changed by any other edit window and therefore overwrite the value of the Snapshot. (except for the parameters in a Slider Widget).

- **Managing Rigs/Widgets**

  - **Remove Widgets from Rigs**: Use the delete command from the Edit Menu or Shortcut Menu or just hit the delete Key.

  - **Show Widget Assignment**: Any Parameter that is assigned to a Widget displays the little Rig icon next to its value.

  - **Reveal Widget:** Ctr+click on a "rigged" Parameter and select the Reveal Widget "*widget name*" form the Shortcut Menu (or Animation menu) to switch the Inspector to display that Widget.

  - **Reveal Target Parameter:** Ctr+click on the Target Parameter and select the command Reveal Target Parameter from the Shortcut Menu (or Animation menu) to have the Object selected the Target Parameter belongs to. This switches the Inspector to display that Parameter. The parameter name will flash yellow for a few seconds so you can spot it better.

  Reveal Target Parameter

  - **Remove Target Parameter from Widget**: Ctr+click on the Target Parameter and select Remove from Widget ... on the Shortcut Menu (or the Animation menu). This command is also available in the Inspector for any Parameter that has been assigned to a Widget, the ones with the Rig icon.

- **Publish Widgets**

Inspector ➤ Project

To "Publish a Parameter" means, making that Parameter available for editing in FCPx when you export a Motion Project as a FCPx Template. You can publish virtually any single Parameter, but it is more powerful to publish Widgets because you can either combine several Parameter in one controller or limit the available options for a control. The Project Inspector displays all the published controls (Parameter Controls and Widget Controls). You can use this window as yet another convenient Editing Window. The Animation menu lets you "Unpublish" parameters and also reveal their origin.

All the Motion tools we've covered so far can create amazing motion effects with surprising ease of use. However, this is just scratching the surface of Motion's potential. Now let's enter another dimension and explore the 3D world with even more tools and possibilities that will really take your Project to new levels.

As usual, when I enter a new topic, I like to answer and clarify the important questions first. In this Chapter: **What does all that 3D and Camera stuff mean?** Again, we have to start with the fundamentals, to understand the underlying concepts, before moving anything around in 3D.

First step, when talking about 2D and 3D (and not just in Motion), we have to be clear on two elements:
The Viewer and The Space.

➡ **Space:**
The Space is the environment where you place Objects. The space can be 2-dimensional or 3-dimensional.

3-dimensional axis

- **2D**: A piece of paper or a computer screen is a 2-dimensional space. It is represented by a 2-axis system, width (x) and height (y). Every point in that system can be defined as a x,y coordinate.

- **3D**: A real three dimensional model has an additional axis, depth (z). Now, with x,y,z coordinates, you can define any point in a 3-dimensional space.

But even in a 2-dimensional space, it is a common practice to "fake" the third dimension with drawing techniques that simulate the 3D space with an optical illusion. That is also what we are doing in Motion when creating 3D Compositions because the Motion Project is after all a "real life" 2D space (on your computer screen) where you create a "virtual" 3D space.

➡ **Viewer:**
This element is often overlooked and taken for granted in the context of 2D vs 3D. However, to fully understand the difference between 2D and 3D and their related tools in Motion, it is very important to keep the viewer in mind. The Viewer is the actual observer (which is you) looking at the Space containing the Objects.

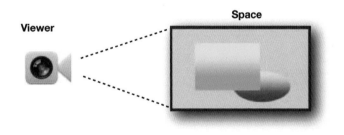

Now with these two elements, the Viewer and the Space, think about what is it that creates movement or motion.

💡 **The Viewer is stationary and the Objects in the Space are moving**

For example, you (the Viewer) stand still and you look at cars (Objects in Space) moving by. From your view point, the cars are getting closer and then further away.

💡 **The Objects in Space are stationary and the Viewer is moving**

For example, cars on a street (Objects in Space) are stationary and you (the Viewer) run by. From your view point, the stationary cars are getting closer and then further away.

💡 **Viewer and Objects are moving**

Of course, both elements can move at the same time.

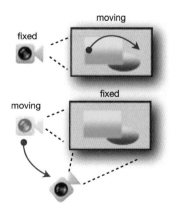

The most important thing about 3D Composition in Motion is to understand that it is not one switch that enables you to do 3D Compositions. There are no 2D Projects or 3D Projects. However, there are different "levels of 3D" in your Project.

Think about three levels based on the elements *Viewer* and *Objects:*

☑ **Level 1 - Basic 3D Tools**: Work on Objects in Space

Motion provides basic 3D tools that let you work with your Objects in 3D space.

☑ **Level 2 - Extended 3D Tools**: Work on Objects in Space (extended tools)

Motion provides extended 3D tools that give you more options to work with your Objects in a 3D space.

☑ **Level 3 - Camera:** Work on different Viewers

Motion provides Objects called Cameras that let you work in 3D space by changing the "Viewer".

Some Objects have Parameters, labeled "3D" or "Camera", that affect their 3D behaviors (Text, Particles, Replicator). They will add additional modules or parameters when activated to work in 3D space.

Basic 3D Tools

This is the first level of working in 3D. We are not changing the Viewer, it is still stationary. We are changing the Objects in our 2D space to make them appear that they are in a 3D space. Here are the various controls.

▶ **Parameter Values (Inspector, HUD)**

Remember that the 3D space has one more coordinate, the z-axis, the depth in space. So every Parameter that has a z-value in addition to the x and y value can be adjusted in a 3D space. Many Compound Parameters (a control with a disclosure triangle) that includes x,y,z coordinates as its Sub-Parameters is one of those controls.

Here is an example from the Transform module in the Inspector's Properties tab. The Position and Rotation parameters include all three axis when you expand the disclosure triangle. This enables you to position or rotate that Object in 3D space.

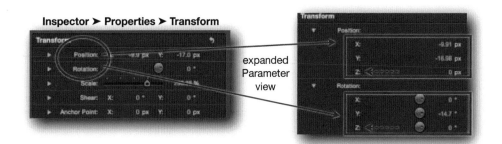

▶ **3D Control Buttons (HUD)**

We've already covered the Transform Tool and the 3D Transform Tool. This is another example of basic 3D tools.

When you select the 3D Transform Tool, the HUD extends its window to provide additional 3D control buttons. Click on a button and drag the mouse to adjust the selected Object in 3D space.

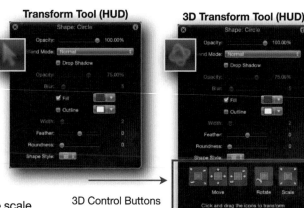

🔵 **Move:** These three buttons let you move the selected Object either along the z-axis, the x and y axis, or the x and z axis.

🔵 **Rotate:** This button lets you rotate the selected Object around the x, y and z axis.

🔵 **Scale:** This button lets you scale the Object. It duplicated the scale slider in the Inspector and is not necessarily a 3D control, unless you imitate distance in space by changing the size of an Object

‣ **Onscreen Controls (Canvas)**

If the 3D Transform Tool is selected, the onscreen controls in the Canvas will also change.

- The arrows ❶ move the Object along the three axis: x - red, y - green, z - blue (remember, the blue dot is the blue arrow looking straight at it (that is from the view point of the Viewer).
- Dragging the little rotation circles ❷ will rotate the Object around the three rotation axis ❸.

   Here is an example where the two objects (circle and text) are lined up flat ❹ in the first picture. The second picture has the text rotated around the y=axis, so it appears that it is coming towards you ❺.

**3D Transform Tool
Onscreen Control**

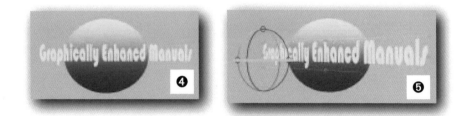

Of course, all these parameters and controls can be animated with Keyframes or Behaviors. This provides a wide variety of tools to create a cool 3D composition without entering any special 3D mode. Also, the Viewer is stationary the whole time, looking straight at the 2D space that is simulating the 3D space. It only transforms the Objects.

Extended 3D Tools

This is the second level in 3D compositing that provides more tools and modified behaviors with a special 3D mode.

> **Group - 3D mode**

Now, we are actually switching from a 2D mode to a 3D mode. However, the switching mode doesn't affect the whole Project. This is the concept:

- 💡 Only a Group Layer can be switched between 2D and 3D.
- 💡 Each Group Layer can be switched individually.
- 💡 The 2D/3D mode affects only the Image Layers inside that Group Layer.

2D Group Layer

Click to toggle
2D - 3D

3D Group Layer

Click to toggle
2D - 3D

The mode can be toggled with any of those 4 commands:

- Click the Group icon ❻ (the black and white one) in the Layers List
- Select the Group and choose Inspector ➤ Group ➤ Group Controls Type. The Type popup menu provides two options: 2D/3D ❼
- Select the Group(s) and use the Main Menu Command Object ➤ 3D Group
- Select the Group(s) and use the Key Command ctr+D

Inspector ➤ Group

Properties   Behaviors   Filters   Group

Group Controls

Type: 2D ⬍
Fixed Resolution:
Fixed Width: 720.0
Fixed Height: 480.0

2D
✓ 3D ❼

Inspector ➤ Group

Properties   Behaviors   Filters   Group

Group Controls

Type: 3D ⬍
Flatten:
Layer Order:

The Group Inspector window displays different Parameters when set to 2D or 3D.

▶ **Change in the Inspector**

When you switch between 2D and 3D for a Group Layer, the available modules in the Properties tab will change too.

For the Group Layer, the Drop Shadow, Four Corner and Crop disappear and two new modules are available: *Lighting* and *Reflection*.

Which modules are affected depends on the Object type. Here is an example for the Shape Object: It adds three new modules to the Properties tab: *Lighting*, *Shadows* and *Reflection*.

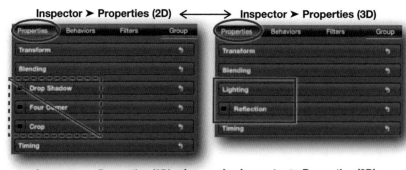

▶ **Change in the Layers Behavior**

There is one important change in behavior when switching a Group Layer to 3D and that affects the stacking order of the Objects inside that Group.

💡 **Layer Order**

The Layers List has a stacking order from top to bottom that determines which Object is visible. The top Layer covers the next Layer below when they are placed in the same space, or the same "plane" (called *coplanar*), like a bunch of pictures laid out on a table. Even if you transform an Object in 3D and create some depth to it (i.e. text pointing into the back of the virtual space), It will still be placed in front of the next Object blow it ❶.

💡 **Depth Order**

If you switch a Group Layer to 3D, then the stacking order of the containing Object changes to a natural behavior. Now, when you transform an Object that is pointing towards the back, it will penetrate the underlying Object (depending on its position and orientation) and the rest of the object (text) will be covered, even if it is on top of the stacking order in the Layers List ❷. The rule, what is visible, now follows the "Depth Order" and not the "Layer Order" anymore.

You can overwrite the default Depth Order of a 3D Group in the Inspector's Group Control with the Layer Order checkbox ❸.

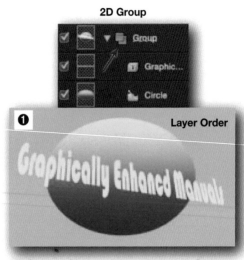

2D Group: Objects follow the Layer Order and don't intersect regardless of their depth.

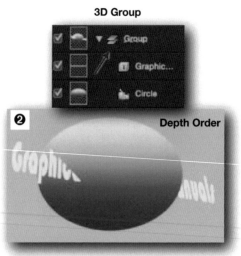

3D Group: Objects ignore the Layer Order and intersect depending on their depth.

Camera

Now we are getting to the third level on how to work in 3D space in Motion. It is very important to be aware of all the various elements that are involved and to understand what happens at every step. Otherwise you can get lost in 3D space very easily and although your Composition looks cool, you might have no idea why and more importantly, can't figure out how to change it in a specific way.

On the first two levels we just covered, we controlled the Object in our Composition while the Viewer stayed stationary (we, the Viewer, looking straight at the Object). Now, we leave the Object stationary and change the Viewer.

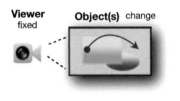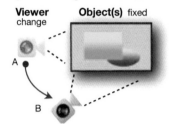

For example, you have two fixed Objects and by changing your position from where you look at those Objects, they appear different (in space). For example:

- **Viewer Position A**: Looking at the Objects from up close and they appear big.
- **Viewer Position B**: Looking at those Objects from far away and the same Objects appear very small.
- **Viewer Position C**: Looking at the Objects from a specific angle where one Object covers the other one and you might see only one Object.

This is the basic concept. But keep in mind that at the moment we are changing to different (stationary) view points to see what our composition looks like from those view points (A, B, or C). We are positioning the Objects in 3D space not by changing the Objects but by changing the view point from where we look at the Object. The position of the Viewer is still stationary at location A, B, or C at a specific time. The next step would be to introduce motion, to move the Viewer gradually from position A to position B. Adding motion later to the Viewer (through Keyframes of Behaviors) works the same as with any other object, but for the moment let's concentrate on the basics of the Viewer and its corresponding tools.

First, we replace the Viewer with a Camera. It is basically the same thing, A Viewer looking through a Camera. As I mentioned before, the default state in Motion (2D or 3D) without any Camera object always implies one Viewer, or one Camera if you will. You, looking straight at the Canvas is the same as a Camera pointed straight at the Canvas and you looking through it. Remember, the reason why the blue arrow on the 3D Transform Tool onscreen control was a dot? Because we looked straight at the z-axis. So let's take it to the next level and create a Camera Object in our Project.

To create a new Camera, use any of these three commands:

- Click on the Camera Icon in the Toolbar
- Use the Main Menu Command Object ➤ New Camera
- Use the Key Command opt+cmd+C

Toolbar

Relationship between Camera Object and 3D mode

If your Project has no Group that is set to 3D when you create a new Camera, then an Alert window will popup with the option to switch the Groups to 3D mode. This will switch all existing Groups to 3D mode.

Camera Rules

- A Camera Object is added as a a Camera Layer in the Layers List.
- You can add as many Camera Objects as you want.
- You can move the Camera Layer to any position in the Layers List. As a Controller Object, it has no affect on other Image Layers.
- A Camera only affects Groups that are set to 3D mode (you can have 2D and 3D Groups in your Projects).
- 2D Groups ignore any Camera parameters. They are viewed from the default position, straight down.

Camera Controls

Once you created the first Camera in your Project, a whole set of new controls become available.

► **Camera Layer**

Any new Camera will always be placed on top of your Layers List (below the Project Layer). Like any other Layer, you can rename it, lock it and drag it to any position in the List.

The checkbox will disable the Camera and all its functions. If no Camera is active, then the Groups in your Project appear in their default Viewer position (looking straight down).

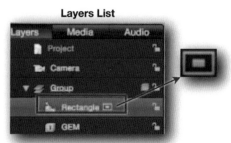

Camera with assigned Behaviors

You can assign special Behaviors to Cameras (Camera Behaviors) to simulate Camera techniques (dolly moves, sweeps, zooms, etc). Those Behaviors will be displayed as a nested Behavior Object Layer underneath the Camera Layer.

Adding a Camera to your Project changes how a selected Image Layer appears in the Layers List. Now an additional Canvas icon is displayed next to any selected Camera or Image Layer. See the related *Isolate* function later in the chapter.

Layers List

► **Camera Inspector / HUD**

The Parameters for a Camera can be displayed in the Inspector and the HUD as with any other Object.

The Camera tab in the Inspector contains the *Camera Controls* module and the *Depth of Field* module to set the basic attributes of the camera. The Properties tab contains the *Transform* module that defines the Camera's placement in space (also controlled by Canvas and HUD onscreen controls) and the *Timing* module that defines its placement in time (corresponds to the placement of the Camera Clip on the Timeline).

The HUD displays the main Camera parameters plus the 5 control buttons to move the Camera in 3D space. These are the controls, usually available when the 3D Transform Tool is selected. And actually, when selecting a Camera, the Tools in the Toolbar automatically switch to the 3D Transform Tools. All other Tools in the Toolbar are grayed out. However, when you switch to a Camera, the HUD displays only the Parameters and you have to click on the 3D Transform Tool again to extend the HUD display to reveal the buttons.

► **Camera Onscreen Controls**

Most changes happen in the Canvas when adding a Camera. Additional onscreen menus and controls pop up. Here is a quick overview before going into details:

Camera Menu

3D View Tools

Canvas

View Menu

3D Compass

Inset View

❶ Camera Menu: The menu lets you choose the Camera that is "looking at the Canvas" plus some often used commands. You have to understand the concept of the two different camera types used in Motion. Otherwise what's going on in the Canvas will be very confusing.

    💡 **Scene Cameras:**

        A Scene Camera is any Camera that you created in your Project. The *Active Camera* is the one Scene Camera the Playhead is currently positioned at in the Timeline.

    💡 **Reference Cameras:**

        A Reference Camera is a temporary Camera that you use to look at your composition from a specific angle. This camera is provided by Motion and is not an Object of your Project like the Scene Cameras.

❷ 3D View Tools: The first icon, the Camera, is not a button, just a display. It is visible if you are currently looking at the Canvas through any Scene Camera. The other three icons function as buttons that you can drag to move the Camera (or the Object) that is displayed in the Camera Menu. It works in a way that is similar to the 3D Transform buttons in the HUD to position the Camera. Double+click on any button will reset the Position and Rotation of the current Camera.

❸ View Menu: This menu is visible regardless of a Camera Object. It contains the 3D view options. Now, when working in the 3D space, you select which 3D Overlays you want to see. The *Show 3D Overlay* command toggles the selection on-off. Remember that those options are also available in the Main Menu under View, and some options also have Key Commands.

❹ Inset View: This is a picture-in-picture feature that is only visible under the following circumstances: Usually, the Canvas displays the view of the camera that you are adjusting. What if you want to position a selected camera, but the Canvas displays the view of a different camera selected in the Camera Menu? In that case, the Inset View shows the view of that selected Camera you are adjusting. When adjusting an Object, the Inset View displays a perspective view of just that Object.

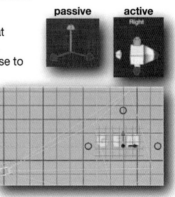

passive   active

❺ 3D Compass: This is an orientation tool that displays the three axis and helps you see what angle you are viewing the Objects from when you rotate the Camera. This is the *passive state*. When you move your mouse over the Compass, it changes into an *active state* that you can use to switch to different Reference Camera without going to the Camera Menu's popup menu.

❻ 3D Grid: Remember that in a 2D space the Grid in the Canvas represents the area of the x,y axis. In 3D mode, the Grid represents the area of the x,z axis. That means, when the camera points directly "into" the z axis, you won't see the Grid.

❼ 3D Scene Icons (not visible in the screenshot above): Those icons (cameras, light and guides) that are visible under specific circumstances, can be used as onscreen controls.

Scene Camera - Reference Camera

Let's have a closer look at those two different camera types.

Scene Camera

Here is an example of a Project with three Cameras displayed at the top of the Layers List. Those same three Cameras will be listed in the (dynamic) Camera Menu.

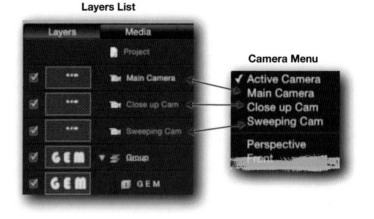

Active Camera (current Scene Camera)

Technically this is also a Scene Camera selection, a dynamic selection, depending on the position of the Playhead. Here is another example of a Project with three Cameras. You can see on the Video Timeline how you can switch between different Cameras. If you were In FCPx, you would place three Clips on the Timeline representing the three shots from three different Cameras. Now think of it as if you placed three Clips on the Motion Timeline. Each one represents one of the three Cameras (their view point) that creates the visuals of your Objects in "real time". When the Camera Menu is set to "Active Camera", Motion will display in the Canvas whatever Scene Cameras is at the current Timeline position. You can overlap the Camera Clips, however, they have their own Camera stacking order. The Camera on top always has priority.

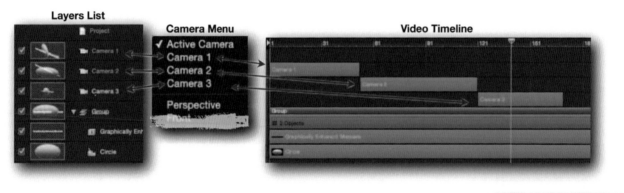

If any Scene Camera is selected, the 3D View Tool will display the Camera icon.

Reference Camera:

A Reference Camera is a temporary Camera view created by Motion that lets you view your Composition from a specific angle. For example, look at the Objects from the front, from the back, from the left, etc. This lets you quickly check your Composition from different angles. Those Reference Cameras are also called "orthographic cameras", which means looking straight down at one axis.

Imagine you have three cameras mounted on your set that record your Scene (the Scene Cameras). In addition to that, you have mounted 6 view finders that point at your set from different angles (front, back, top, etc). While your actor is performing the scene, you can go to any of those view finders (Reference Cameras) and see how the scene looks from that angle. Please note that although positioned at a specific angle, you can move those Reference Cameras in the Canvas with the 3D View Tools. If a Reference Camera has been moved from its original position, then it will have a little asterisk added after its name. Double+click on any of the three 3D View Tool buttons to reset the Reference Camera to its default position.

Original
Reference Camera

modified
Reference Camera

Here is an example that helps to demonstrate the Reference Cameras:

I created a Project with six Text Objects and three Circle Objects. I aligned the Text Objects in the 3D space along the x, y and z axes so they are correctly readable when viewed from a straight 90° angle. Their colors refer to the color coded axes they are looked at. The three circles are aligned at the crosspoint of all three axes. They are also colored so you can see what axes you are looking "into".

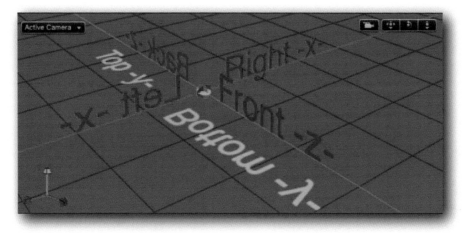

Please compare the views with the orientation of the 3D Compass. The 3D Compass is your friend in 3D space. It might take a little practice and imagination at first to take advantage of that helpful tool.

Looking straight from the Front or Back at the Composition means looking straight down the z-axis (blue). Only the blue objects are visible. The other objects are also there, but looked at straight from the side and therefore are visible only as lines.

Looking straight from the Left or Right at the Composition means looking straight into the x-axis (red). The other objects are again only visible as lines from that angle (the Objects are two-dimensional without depth).

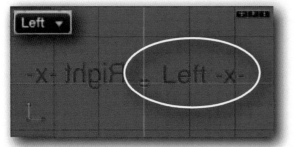 

Looking straight from the Top or Bottom at the Composition means looking straight into the y-axis (green). The other objects are again only visible as lines from that angle..

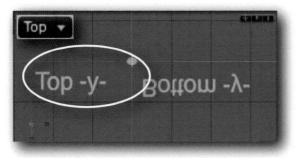 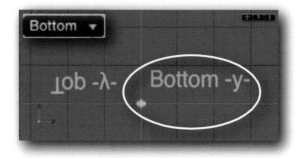

The View, The Active and The Selected

Let's pause for a moment.

I just gave an overview of the Camera Objects and the available controls. We could continue to dive into the details, see what happens when we apply those Objects and techniques in our Project. However, this can get very complex and potentially confusing with all the parameters, conditions and Canvas views. And the more you have going on in your Project, the higher the chance that you'll get lost.

Let me try to present an easy tool to always stay on top of what is going on in your Composition when working with cameras in the 3D space regardless how complex your Project is. I call it, *"The View, The Active and The Selected"*.

Whenever you work in your Project, actively adjusting Objects or just monitoring the Canvas, double check on those three states to make sure that you know what you are looking at and know what you are adjusting. Your decision is based on the combination of those three states:

 View

Look at the **Canvas**

The first question is, what am I seeing in the Canvas. When a Project has no Cameras, the answer is simple. The Canvas displays the state of your Composition at the current time displayed in the Time Display which represents the position of the Playhead in the Timeline. We <u>view</u> it through an "imaginary" camera that points directly at the Canvas (x,y).

After adding the first Camera to a Project, a lot of new onscreen options are available in the Canvas and the answer to "what are we looking at?" is shown in one of those new menus, the Camera Menu in the upper left corner of the Canvas. These are the available (but not all) options:

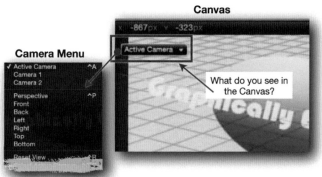

- **Active Camera**: You view the Canvas through the Scene Camera based on the Playhead position. In the previous example with the three Cameras, the Canvas would switch from Camera 1 to Camera 2 to Camera 3 when you play the whole Project.

- **Scene Cameras**: These are the individual Camera Objects in your Project. They are listed in the Camera Menu below the Active Camera. Selecting a Scene Camera will only show that camera view in the Canvas and will not switch to a different Active Camera based on the Playhead position (any Behaviors added to that Scene Camera however will play at its timing position).
  Think of this setting in the following way. While you are playing your composition, everything is performing as programed (moving and changing Objects). You just view everything through that one Scene Camera and ignore any instructions to switch to a different Scene Camera.

- **Reference Cameras**: Same principle here. Your Composition still performs as programmed when you play it but this time you view it through one of those Reference Cameras. The middle section in the Camera Menu displays all the available Reference Cameras. Remember, they are not part of your Project.

➡ **Isolate**

This is a function in Motion that is related to the question of 'what is visible' in the Canvas.

Selecting a Scene Camera or a Reference Camera from the Camera Menu overwrites the standard 'Active Camera' view. As we have just seen, these options *isolate* a specific view and display that view in the Canvas instead of the 'Active Camera' view. However there is an additional Camera view that can be isolated and displayed in the Canvas.

Think of a Camera that you have available which you can point directly at any single Image Layer available in your Layers List (even Groups). This way you can view that Layer 'isolated' from all the rest of your objects, Cameras and that Layer's own position in the 3D space. That is what the Canvas displays during that state. The Camera Menu in the upper left corner displays the name of the isolated Layer even if that item is not part of the Camera Menu.

So there are a total of three types of items that can be viewed, isolated in the Canvas:

- **Scene Camera**: Selectable from the Camera Menu or with the Isolate command
- **Reference Camera**: Selectable from the Camera Menu only.
- **Image Layer**: Selectable with the Isolate command only.

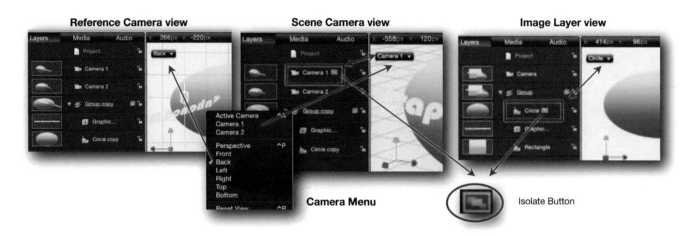

Reference Camera view   **Scene Camera view**   **Image Layer view**

Camera Menu   **Isolate Button**

These are the Isolate commands that can be used for the Scene Camera and Image Layer:

- Select the Object in the Layers List and choose the Main Menu command: Object ➤ Isolate
- Select the Object in the Layers List and choose the Key Command ctrl+I
- Click on the Canvas icon next to the Object in the Layers List. Remember, when you have at least one Camera in your Project, every selected Object will display that little Canvas icon in the Layers List. Click on that icon to toggle between selected and isolated.

selected ⟷ isolated

And here is the reason why it is important to know what is the current *View* in the Canvas: The buttons of the 3D View Tools in the upper right corner of the Canvas control the Object(s) that is "viewing" the Canvas. The buttons don't control the Active Camera or the Selected Camera, only the Camera (or Image Layer) with the current "view". That's why the buttons are called '3D **View** Tools'.

Canvas

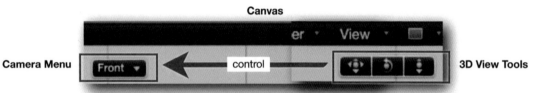

Camera Menu   Front ▼   ⟵ control ⟶   **3D View Tools**

So be aware: Adjusting a Scene Camera changes the position of that Camera in your Composition and therefore the look of your Composition. Adjusting a Reference Camera on the other hand has no affect on your Composition. You just look at it from a different angle, and you would only adjusting that viewing angle.

💡 **Active**

Look at the **Timeline**

This state comes down to one simple question. At what position is the Playhead at the moment? You look at the Timeline pane and see what Camera Clip the Playhead is currently crossing over. That is the Active Camera. In the example to the right, it is Camera 3.
There are three basic scenarios:

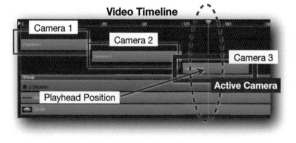

- **Project has no Cameras**: The Active Camera is always the default view looking straight at the Canvas.
- **Project has one Camera**: The Active Camera is always that one Camera. The Camera Clip in the Timeline spans from the beginning to the end of the Project.
- **Project has multiple Cameras**: The Active Camera changes depending on the position of the Playhead.

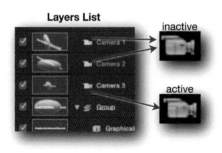

There are two more indicators for the Active Camera in the Layers List. The little camera icon will have an added red Record LED to indicate when a Camera becomes the Active Camera. All the names of the non-active Cameras are dimmed. Please note that these indicators are not dynamically updated when you play your Project. They change only when you pause of jump to a new time position.

Selected

Look at the **Layers List**

This is the third question in our checklist, a simple one: What Object(s) is currently selected? We already know all the techniques for selecting Object and how to recognize which Object is selected.

- **Select an Object**: Click on the Object in the Layers List, the Timeline or the Canvas.
- **Recognize a selected Object**:
  - The Object in the Layers List is highlighted and has the little Canvas icon (when you have at least one Camera in your Project).
  - The Object Clip in the Timeline is highlighted.
  - The Object has its onscreen controls visible in the Canvas based on the currently selected Tool.

And here is the simple reason why it is important to know what Object is selected: The Inspector and the HUD control the selected Object(s).

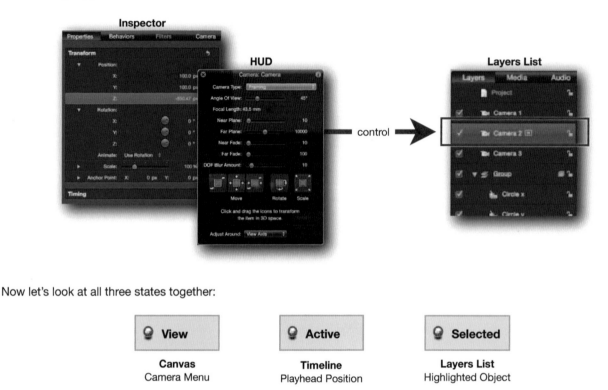

Now let's look at all three states together:

View	Active	Selected
Canvas	**Timeline**	**Layers List**
Camera Menu	Playhead Position	Highlighted Object

Of course in a project with multiple cameras, the situation is most likely a combination of those three states. One Camera could provide the current View but is not the Active Camera and a different Camera is selected at the same time. This is the complexity I was talking about earlier. Here are some rules based on two important questions:

What controls what?
- The 3D View Tools always control the **View** Camera (or Object)
- The Inspector and HUD always control the **Selected** Camera
- Onscreen Controls are visible and controlling the **Selected** Camera

What is displayed in the Canvas?
- Any **Selected** Camera (or Object) that is not the **View** Camera is displayed in the Inset View during editing.
- Any **Selected** Camera that is not the **View** Camera is displayed as a white camera icon with guides.
- The **Active** Camera that is not the **View** Camera is displayed as a yellow camera icon.

To demonstrate those rules, I created a Project with three Cameras and made every possible combination for the View, Active and Selected state. This is the setup:

- The **View** Camera (selected in the Camera Menu) is always Camera 1 (C1). The Camera View menu reads "Camera 1".

- The **Active** Camera is Camera 1 in the first row, Camera 2 in the second row and Camera 3 in the third row. I moved the Playhead in the Timeline over C1 (1st row), over C2 (2nd row) and then over C3 (3rd row).

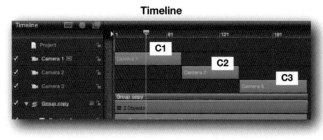

Timeline

- The **Selected** Camera in my setup is Camera 1 in the first column. The three screenshots in the second columns have Camera 2 selected and the screenshots in the third column have Camera 3 selected.

The screenshots are a little small but I hope it will answer the question about 'what controls what' and 'what is displayed'.

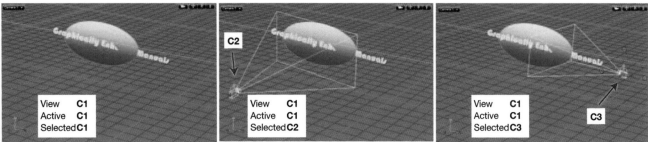

View C1 Active C1 Selected C1	C2 ↓ View C1 Active C1 Selected C2	View C1 Active C1 Selected C3 C3

C1: Use 3D View tools

C1: Use 3D View tools
C2: Use white onscreen controls (plus Inspector and HUD) - Inset View

C1: Use 3D View tools
C3: Use white onscreen controls (plus Inspector and HUD) - Inset View

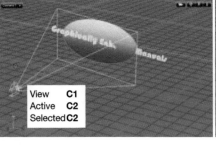
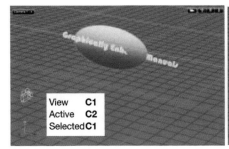

View C1 Active C2 Selected C1	View C1 Active C2 Selected C2	View C1 Active C3 Selected C3

C1: Use 3D View tools
C2: camera displayed in yellow

C1: Use 3D View tools
C2: Use yellow onscreen controls (plus Inspector and HUD) - Inset View

C1: Use 3D View tools
C2: camera displayed in yellow
C3: Use white onscreen controls (plus Inspector and HUD) - Inset View

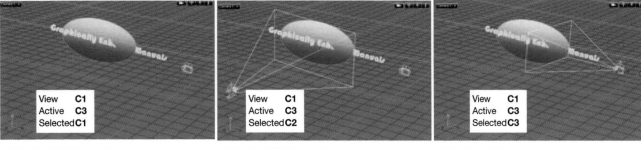

View C1 Active C3 Selected C1	View C1 Active C3 Selected C2	View C1 Active C3 Selected C3

C1: Use 3D View tools
C3: camera displayed in yellow

C1: Use 3D View tools
C2: Use white onscreen controls (plus Inspector and HUD) - Inset View
C3: camera displayed in yellow

C1: Use 3D View tools
C3: yellow onscreen controls (plus Inspector and HUD) - Inset View

The View Camera (Camera 1 in my example) is never visible as a camera icon in the Canvas because you are looking through that Camera. What you see in the Canvas is the result of the position and the parameters of that View Camera.

Whenever you use the onscreen controls (selected Object), the Inset View will be displayed in the lower right corner (depending on additional Preferences settings).

➡ **Inset View**

The Inset View is automatically activated under two circumstances:

❶ **When you edit a "non-View" camera**:

Let me repeat it again. A "View" Scene Camera (i.e. C1), a camera that is selected in the Camera Menu doesn't need an Inset View. You are viewing through that Camera (C1) in the Canvas, the 'Main View". Any changes to that camera will be visible in the Canvas right away. However, if you select a Camera (C2) that is not the View Camera and you edit it (change its position), you would not see the effect because the Canvas displays the viewpoint of a different Camera (C1).

This is what the Inset View is for. When you adjust the selected Camera (C2), the Inset View pops up, displaying the viewpoint of the selected Camera (C2) in that little picture-in-picture window.

❷ **When you edit an Image Layer**

The Inset View is not only for different Cameras. When you edit any Image Layer in your Composition, the Inset View will also pop up. This time the viewpoint is from the perspective Reference Camera. For example, if you are zoomed in very closely on an Object that you are adjusting, the perspective Reference Camera uses a zoom level to display all the Objects so you can see your adjustments in a better context.

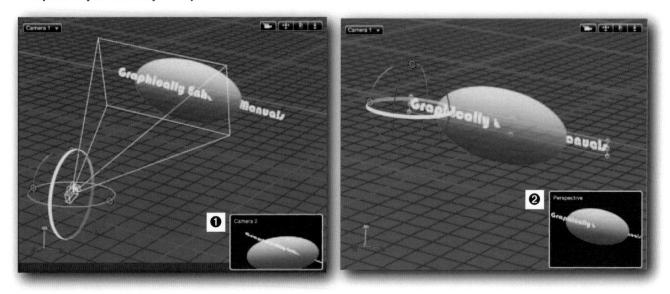

◯ The Inset View will be visible while you do the adjustments (mouse clicked).

◯ The Inset View will pop up, not only if you use the onscreen controls, but also if you use the Inspector or HUD controls.

◯ The Inset View displays the name of the Camera who's viewpoint it's displaying.

◯ You can change the size of the Inset View and its behavior in the Preferences. For example, keep the window visible all the time (Manually) or let it pop up when doing any changes or transform changes only.

➡ **Tip**

When switching between Camera views and doing adjustments of the Cameras or other Objects, you may find yourself constantly zooming in and out and repositioning the frame you are viewing. There are two controls that makes that maneuvering much easier and faster.

Reposition the frame

Space+drag: When you hold down the space key on your keyboard while dragging the Canvas, you actually move the Project frame in your Canvas. Depending on your available screen real estate, this lets you quickly position the frame to better adjust the Objects in the frame.

Zoom in-out

Two-finger pinch: If you have a Track Pad, use this simple gesture over the Canvas to quickly zoom in and out of your Project frame.

Remember, both commands won't affect your Composition, only the Canvas view.

➡ **Controls**

Motion provides a wide variety of controls in different windows. Although many of the controls that affect the position of an Object in space (Transform) affect the same parameters, they have different labels. Here is an overview of all those controllers and how they are related.

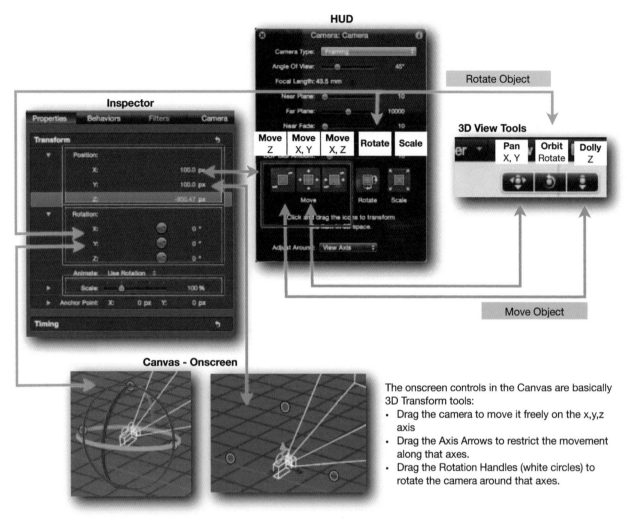

The onscreen controls in the Canvas are basically 3D Transform tools:
- Drag the camera to move it freely on the x,y,z axis
- Drag the Axis Arrows to restrict the movement along that axes.
- Drag the Rotation Handles (white circles) to rotate the camera around that axes.

Remember the Key Commands for the 3D Transform tools:

Moving the mouse over a Rotation Handle makes the Rotation Axis visible. The rotation is restricted to that axis.

Holding down the command key: move the mouse into the inner circle and then drag to rotate freely around all axis. Any rotation axis will turn yellow when the mouse is moved over it. This indicates that the rotation is now restricted to that axis (while still pressing down the command key).

▶ **Adjust Around**

At the bottom of the HUD is a popup menu labeled "Adjust Around". This defines the axis that you move the object around.

- **World Axis**: This is the main 3D grid in the Canvas that relates to the 3D Compass.
- **Local Axis**: This refers to the axis of the selected Object.
- **View Axis**: This orients the selected object around the space of the current view.

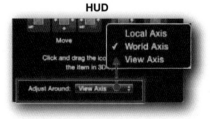

► **Camera Type**

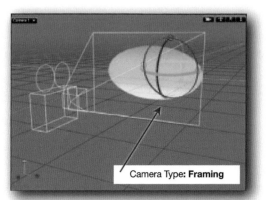

I don't want to go into the details of all the Camera Controls. However, let me point out the importance of the very first parameter, the Camera Type.

On the previous pages, I explained how to move the camera with the onscreen controls. You may have noticed that a selected Camera is displayed in the Canvas not only as the camera but also with the projection of the frame it is "filming". The Camera type parameter provides two options for moving the camera:

- 💡 **Viewpoint**: The transform controls are attached to the camera. This uses the camera as the anchor point
- 💡 **Framing**: The transform controls are attached to the frame. It uses that frame as the anchor point

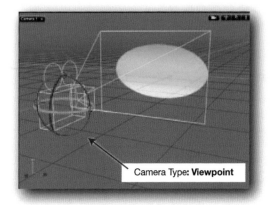

Camera Type: **Viewpoint** Camera Type: **Framing**

Viewports

Canvas - Layout Menu

The menu at the upper right corner of the Canvas is the Layout Menu. I discussed it briefly in the Canvas chapter. This menu lets you choose from seven different view layouts which are different arrangements of up to four viewports. Each viewport can be set to a different View Camera. They all display your Composition at the current Playhead position allowing you to check the same position in your Composition from different camera views.

► **Selected Viewport**

All the aspects of our cameras, what we see and what we control, apply to each individual viewport. Just click on the frame (viewport) and it will get a yellow border around it. When you play your Composition, only the selected viewport is playing it live from its camera's viewpoint (Scene Camera or Reference Camera). Also, only the active viewport can be edited.

Please not that the rest of the Canvas View Menus (Zoom, Color, Render, View) are affecting each viewport individually. That means you can set those options differently for each (selected) viewport.

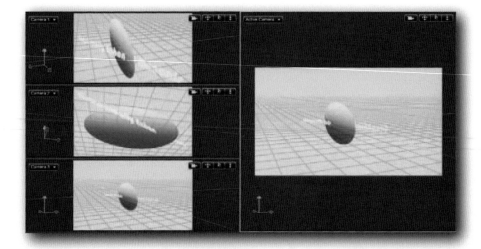

Light

So far we've covered the 3D topic going through the three levels, Basic 3D, Extended 3D and Cameras. Here are a few more elements that provide additional features and tools to make the 3D Composition even more realistic, starting with proper lighting.

A Light is just another Control Object that you add to your Project.

To create a new Light, use any of these three commands:

- Click on the Light Icon in the Toolbar
- Use the Main Menu Command Object ➤ New Light
- Use the Key Command sh+cmd+L

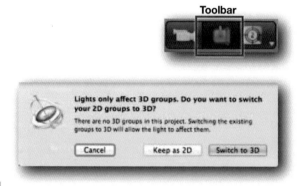

Relationship between a Light Object and 3D mode

If your Project has no Group that is set to 3D when you create a new Light, an Alert window will pop up with the option to switch the Groups to 3D mode. This will switch all existing Groups to 3D mode.

Please note that you could use only a Light Object and no Camera Object in your Project and still have all the 3D Camera menus and controls available in the Canvas. This just uses the (invisible) default Camera pointing straight at your Project.

▶ **Light Rules**

- A Light Object is added as a Light Layer in the Layers List.
- You can add as many Light Objects as you want.
- You can move the Light Layer to any position in the Layers List. As a Controller Object, it has no affect on other Image Layers.
- A Light only has an affect on Groups that are set to 3D mode (you can have 2D and 3D Groups in your Projects).
- 2D Groups ignore any Light parameters. The default Light is an invisible Ambient Light.
- Light has a color attribute.

▶ **Inset View**

Adjusting any Light Object will also pop up an Inset View in the Canvas that displays the view through the perspective Reference Camera.

▶ **Reaction to Light**

Adding a Light Object is only half the story. The question is, what effect does it have on existing Objects. The answer is, it depends. Switching a Group to 3D mode adds an additional *Lighting* module in its Inspector and to all its included Objects. The Shading Parameter in this module determines how the Object reacts to light.

Inspector ➤ Properties

- Shading **On**: The Object reacts to Light.
- Shading **Off**: The Object does not react to Light.
- Shading **Inherited**: This inherits the Lighting setting of its parent Group.

The Highlight parameter with its Shininess slider controls whether or not the Object shows highlights on its surface and how strong they are, creating a glossy effect.

▶ **Render Lighting**

Lighting effects could use up a lot of CPU power. If you think that your playback is negatively impacted, disable Lighting rendering from the Canvas Render menu.

Light Controls

Once you've created the first Camera in your Project, new controls become available.

▶ **Light Layer**

Any new Light will always be placed on top of your Layers List below any Camera Layer. Like any other Layer, you can rename it, lock it and drag it to any position in the List.

The checkbox will disable the Camera and all its functions. You're literally "turning off the light". Your Motion Project returns to its default ambient light when all the Light Objects are turned off.

Light with assigned Behaviors

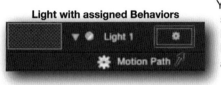

You can assign Behaviors to Lights to simulate moving light techniques. Those Behaviors will be displayed as nested Behavior Objects underneath with an additional Behavior Icon on the Light Layer.

Remember, if you select any Image Layer in the Layers List, the Canvas icon will be placed next to the Object name to indicate that it is selected and available as an onscreen control in the Canvas. The Light Object however will not display that icon, although it is displaying its onscreen controls in the Canvas when selected.

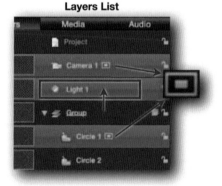

Layers List

▶ **Light Inspector / HUD**

The Parameters for a Light can be displayed in the Inspector and the HUD as with any other Object.

The Light tab in the Inspector contains the *Light Controls* module and the *Shadows* module to set the basic attributes of the light. The available attributes are changing depending on the Light Type. The Properties tab contains the *Transform* module that defines the Light placement in space (also controlled by Canvas and HUD onscreen controls) and the *Timing* module that defines its placement in time (corresponds to the placement of the Light Clip on the Timeline).

The HUD displays the main Light parameters plus the 5 control buttons to move the Light in 3D space. These are the controls, usually available when the 3D Transform Tool is selected. And actually, when selecting a Light, the Tools in the Toolbar automatically switch to the 3D Transform Tool. All other Tools in the Toolbar are grayed out. However, when you switch to a Light, the HUD displays only Parameters and you have to click on the 3D Transform Tool again to extend the HUD display.

Light Types

The first parameter in the Lights Control module is the Light Type. From the popup menu, choose one of four light types.

▶ Ambient

This is the default light when no light is selected. However, when using this as a dedicated Light Object, you can set the color and intensity for the light. Ambient light has no onscreen object in the Canvas.

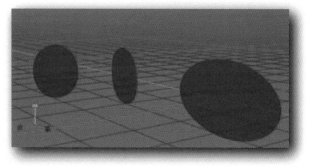

▶ Directional

This type of Light distributes light from its position in one direction. Think of it as one big endless wall that emits light.

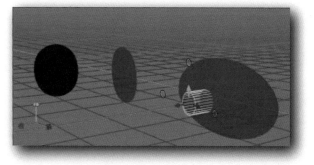

▶ Point

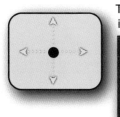

This type of light distributes light from one spot into all directions around it in 3D space.

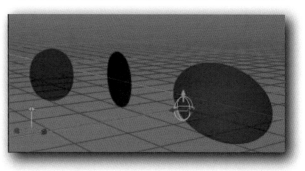

▶ Spot

This type of light distributes light from one spot into a specific directions in 3D like a cone.

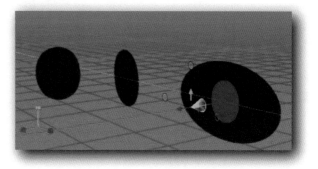

Of course you can use multiple lights in your Composition, position and point them in 3D the same way you would on a real live set.

Shadow - Reflection

Like the Lighting module, Shadow and Reflection are additional modules located in the Inspector ➤ Properties pane that are only available if the Object is part of a 3D Group.

Shadow

The Shadow effect is a "Cast Shadow" that requires a Light Object as the light source in 3D space. The standard *Drop Shadow* effect on the other hand doesn't require 3D mode. It also works in 2D space and simulates a cast shadow without having a light source.

You need three elements for a simple Cast Shadow effect:

1: A light source - 2: An object that casts the shadow - 3: An object that the shadow is cast on

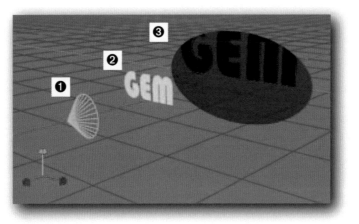

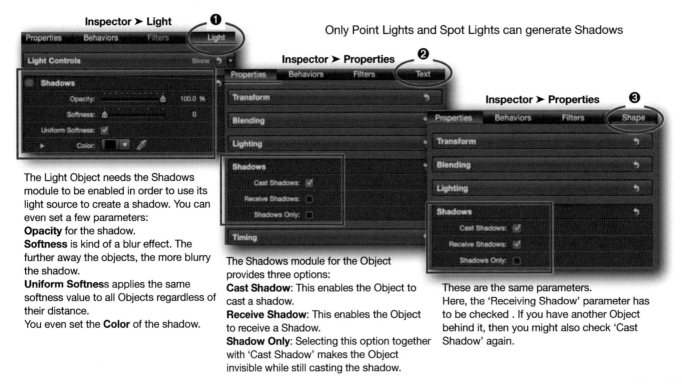

The Light Object needs the Shadows module to be enabled in order to use its light source to create a shadow. You can even set a few parameters:
Opacity for the shadow.
Softness is kind of a blur effect. The further away the objects, the more blurry the shadow.
Uniform Softness applies the same softness value to all Objects regardless of their distance.
You even set the **Color** of the shadow.

The Shadows module for the Object provides three options:
Cast Shadow: This enables the Object to cast a shadow.
Receive Shadow: This enables the Object to receive a Shadow.
Shadow Only: Selecting this option together with 'Cast Shadow' makes the Object invisible while still casting the shadow.

These are the same parameters.
Here, the 'Receiving Shadow' parameter has to be checked . If you have another Object behind it, then you might also check 'Cast Shadow' again.

Of course you can mix your Composition with multiple Lights and shadow casting Objects to create a complex but realistic 3D environment.

Reflection

In real life, when an Object A is close to an Object B that has a very shiny and high reflective surface, then Object A might be visible in Object B. Motion can simulate that effect which is known as *Reflection*.

For a basic Shadow effect you needed three elements (Light - 1. Object - 2. Object). The Reflection effect only needs two elements, Object A that is reflected in Object B. Light is of course necessary to see the effect but it is not required as part of the effect.

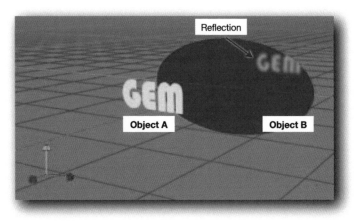

▸ **Object A**

This Object has to be enabled to cast the Reflection. It is done in the Blending module of the Inspector's Properties tab.

▸ **Object B**

The blue bypass button turns the Reflection module on for this Object and its parameters let you adjust the effect.

- **Reflectivity**: Adjust between 0%, no reflection - up to 100%, mirror effect.
- **Blur Amount**: Adjust the focus to simulate the quality of the Object's surface.
- **Falloff - Begin Distance**: Set the distance where the reflection starts to fade.
- **Falloff - End Distance:** Set the distance where the fading of the reflection ends.
- **Exponent**: Set how quickly the fading occurs.
- **Blend Mode**: Select the blend mode that is used for the Reflection Effect.

As with the Lighting, the Rendering for Shadows and Reflections can be disabled individually in the Canvas Render menu.

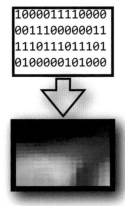

At the beginning of this manual I explained the terms bitmap graphics and vector-based graphics.

Motion can use both types in a Project. However, bitmap graphics are somewhat limited in what you can do with them. Vector-based graphics are way more flexible because they are just computer code instructions that are rendered into an image in real time. Any changes that you apply in Motion to vector images are just changes to the instructions that are then rendered accordingly. As long as you stay with the vector-based graphics, all your options are open.

Render Menu

Once you "flatten" the graphic, you commit to the result and the graphic instructions are converted into pixels/bits that are mapped out over the shape of the image, ending up with a bitmap graphic file that loses most of the options.

So the solution is, never flatten a graphics file and always render in real time. This works unless there are limitations regarding the necessary horsepower of your computer to perform all those realtime render processes.

▶ Render

Motion provides the option to modify certain aspects of the render process in order to use your processing power wisely. The Render menu on top of the Canvas lets you set those options. You can even disable specific CPU intensive tasks like Lighting, Shadow, Motion Blur, etc.

▶ Flatten

Another option is to manually flatten a specific 3D Group with the Flatten checkbox in the Inspector's Group Controls module.

Inspector ➤ Group

▶ Rasterize

The Rasterize function in Motion is also a process that flattens a Group to a bitmap image. However, this process is triggered automatically under certain circumstances.

- 💡 A 2D Group gets rasterized when you edit/use the following features in the Group Inspector:

  Use Drop Shadow, Use Four Corners, use Crop, apply Filters, change Blend modes, adding Masks, adding Light (if the 2D Group is nested in a 3D Group.

- 💡 A 3D Group gets rasterized when you edit/use the following features:

  Use Blend modes (except when in Pass Through mode), use specific Filters, add Light (when the Group is flattened).

A rasterized Group has two indicators to show that it is rasterized:

- 💡 **Rasterization Frame**: This is a frame that surrounds the Group icon in the Layers List.
- 💡 **Rasterization Indicator**: This is a little "R" icon next to the Parameter or module that causes the rasterization.

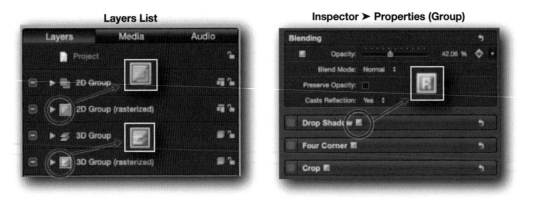

Once a Group is rasterized, it's Objects cannot interact individually with other Objects outside that Group anymore, they act together as one single Object. 3D Emitters, 3D Replicators and Text Objects are treated as 3D Groups for rasterization.

Publish

I discussed most of the Publishing aspects in the chapters about File Management and Rigs. So let me just summarize:

The concept of publishing Projects involves two components:

- 💡 **Publishing a Motion Project as a FCPx Motion Template**

  A Motion Project can be saved as a FCPx Motion Template that can be accessed from inside FCPx and used as one of the four types of Effect Clips: Filter, Transition, Text, Generator.

- 💡 **Publishing Parameters along with that Template**

  Almost any Parameter available in the Motion Project can be "published" as part of the Motion Template. Those published Parameters will then be visible in the FCPx Inspector for that effect and you can adjust the effect with that limited set of "authorized" parameters in your FCPx project.

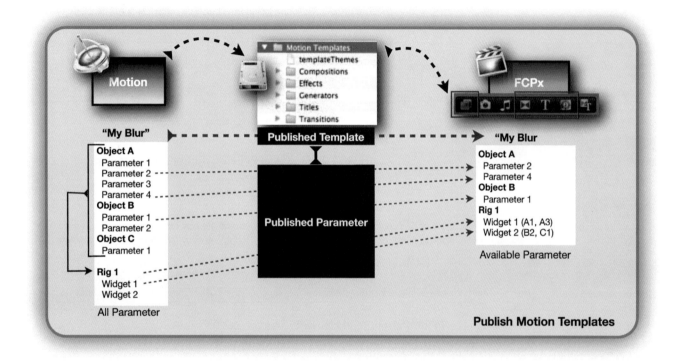

A few things to look out for when publishing parameters:

- 💡 The procedure for publishing single Parameters or Widgets is the same. Just select the Publish command from their Animation Menu. That item will then be displayed in the Project Inspector. You can rename the controls in that window to give it a proper label that makes it clear what it is used for. i.e., you would have two sliders with the name "Opacity" when you publish the opacity parameter for two different Object and wouldn't know which one is which.

- 💡 Some Objects allow you to publish their onscreen controller (OSC) with a checkbox labeled "Publish OSC". This parameter will not be listed as published in the Project Inspector.

- 💡 With Text Objects, you have the option to allow the actual text (and some attributes) to be edited when used in FCPx. The checkbox is labeled "Editable in FCP" in the Inspector ➤ Text ➤ Format ➤ Advanced Formatting.

- 💡 The Drop Zone well of a Drop Zone Layer will automatically be added as a Published Parameter to your Project when you create the Object.

- 💡 There is no true "round-trip" between Motion and FCPx. Whenever you use an Effect in your FCPx Timeline that is based on a Motion Template, that Effect Clip will not be updated when you edit and save that Effect in Motion. In that case, you have to swap the Effect in your FCPx timeline with the new (modified) Motion Effect.

Export

All the export commands are listed under the standard Share Menu. They let you save your Composition to a file format that can be played by a specific application or used for specific purposes.

The functionality of various commands is similar to those in FCPx and Compressor, except:

- The settings window provides a "Duration" menu that lets you choose to export your whole Project or only a section of it defined by the In and Out Markers on the Timeline.
- The settings window has an additional "Render" tab to configure the different aspects on how to render the various processing tasks.

Apple Devices: Those files will be available in iTunes to sync with Apple devices (iPhone, iPad, etc).

DVD / Blu-ray: This lets you create DVD and Blu-ray discs or store a disc image on your drive.

Email: This creates a new email and embeds the exported file, ready to hit the send button.

Share Menu

Apple Devices...
DVD...
Blu-ray...
Email...
YouTube...
Facebook...
Vimeo...
CNN iReport...
Export Movie...   ⌘E
Export Selection to Movie... ⌥⌘E
Export Audio...
Save Current Frame...
Export Image Sequence...
Export for HTTP Live Streaming...
Send to Compressor...
Export using Compressor Settings...
Show Share Monitor

Social Networks: This uploads the file directly to your social media account. The login procedure is performed in the setup window.

Export Movie: cmd+E This is the main Export command.

Export Selection to Movie: opt+cmd+E Exports only the selected Objects in the Layers List.

Export Audio: This saves only the audio tracks of your Project.

Save Current Frame: This creates an image file of the frame the Playhead is currently parked at.

Export Image Sequence: This creates a sequence of images from your Project.

Export for HTTP Live Streaming: Used for Web streaming.

Send to Compressor: This sends a reference file of the Project to Compressor, opens the app and creates a new Job for that Project. Now you can apply any settings to it and let Compressor do the export while you continue to work in FCPx.

Export Using Compressor Settings This opens a window where you can access all the available Compressor settings for exporting. The export is still be handled by Motion in the foreground, which means, you have to wait for it to finish.

Show Share Monitor Opens the Share Monitor application that handles all the rendering of FCPx, Compressor and Motion.

I don't want to go through every parameter in the settings windows, just a few things to be aware of:

- Each export command opens a setup window with a similar user interface (except Send to Compressor).
- The Settings window contains a thumbnail of the Project that lets you skim through the video.
- Each window has up to four tabs: Options - Render - Advanced - Summary.
  Apple Devices has those tabs hidden behind a "Show Details" button.
- The **Options** tab provides all the specific export settings.
- The **Render** tab lets you configure the different aspects on how to render the various processing tasks.
- The **Advanced** tab lists the options for Background Rendering.
  - None: Processing is performed in the foreground.
  - This Computer: Processing is performed in the background on the local machine.
  - This Computer Plus: Processing is performed in the background on a distributed processing cluster (see Compressor for details).
  - Send To Compressor: This "outsources" the processing as a Job to the Compressor app which uses a reference file of the Project.
- The **Summary** tab lists the final properties of the export file.

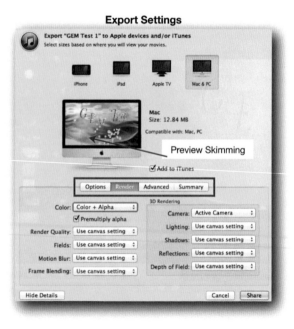

Export Settings

13 - Key Commands

The Key Commands window and its functionality is the same as in FCPx:

💡 **Command**: These are all the commands that Motion lists in the Command section ❶.

💡 **Description**: This is a short description of what the command is for. Select any Command in the Command list and the box next to it will display the Command Details ❷.

💡 **Key Equivalent**: This is the key combination that is assigned to a Command. The Command List has two extra columns where you can see if any Key combination is assigned (Modifiers+Key) ❸.

▸ **Command Sets**: The Key Command Editor is the floating window where you manage those Shortcuts in so called *Command Sets*. Open the window from the Main Menu **Motion ➤ Commands ➤ Customize ...** This will display a virtual Keyboard that represents your connected keyboard (desktop or laptop) and displays a specific Command Set. Please look at the Command Menu. It has a section called "Command Sets" for the built-in Default Sets and the "Custom Command Sets" for all your Customized Sets. You can switch to a different Set at any time. You can also Import and Export Sets if you want to use your Sets on a different computer.

Command Menu

▸ **Filter Commands**: You can filter (restrict) the Command List to display only a specific Command Group ❹ by entering a search string ❺. The magnifying glass icon is actually a popup menu where you can select what you are searching for ❻. Click the Keyboard Highlight button ❼ to highlight Keys that are related to commands that match the search term.

▸ **Key Groups**: This is a great feature. Select any key on the virtual keyboard and the Key Detail list ❽ displays all the possible Modifier Key combinations and the commands that are assigned to that combination. You can drag out any Token (representing the actual Command) from the Key Detail List or drag the Key away from the virtual keyboard ❾ to delete that assignment (in a puff of smoke).

▸ **Add Key Assignment**: Simply select a Command from the Command List and press the key combination on your real keyboard. You will get an alert window if that key assignment is already taken. You can even drag a Key (that is assigned to a command) to a new Key to change the assignment.

▸ **Virtual Keyboard**: The dot on a Key tells you that it has an assignment. The color represents the Command Group (Effect, Editing, etc). A shaded key means that it is off limits due to a System Assignment. The Modifier Keys are slightly darker when selected. They correspond with the modifier buttons at the top ❿.

Key Command Editor

Save Command Set

14 - Preferences

I've already covered many of the Preferences Settings in the various chapters, but here is an overview of the 9 tabs.

▶ General

Startup: Select what happens when you launch Motion. Create a new Project or open the last Project.

Interface: Set the time interval it takes until a Drop Menu will be displayed. Drop Menus are special free floating menus that can pop up during drag-and-drop operations. Usually there is a default behavior (e.g. copy, insert, overwrite) when you release the mouse before the drop menu appears with more options.

The Tooltips window can be disabled with the checkbox.

File Browser & Library: Set the behavior in the File Browser and Library panes. The sort order, the option to display a preview icon in the Stack and the option to automatically play a preview of the selected item in the preview area (or press the play button manually).

Media: When checked, Motion will automatically remove any media file from the Project when you delete the Media Object from the Layers List. When unchecked, Motion keeps the media files (video, audio, graphics) in your Project (in the Media List) in case you want to use them later in your Composition (Layers List).

▶ Appearance

Timeline: Select from the menu what type of label a Clip will display in the Timing Pane.

Canvas: Set the opacity for the part of the Object that extends beyond the Canvas edges (only relevant if *Full View* is enabled).

Thumbnail Preview: Set the background type and color for the little thumbnail preview in the Layers List.

Status Bar: Choose what information is displayed in the Status bar in the left upper corner of the Canvas. Whatever Object your mouse is moving or pointing at, the Status bar will display the selected info. The *Dynamic Tool info* lets you display information while doing Transform edits. The *Display Color As* popup menu provides three display color options, if it was checked.

▶ Project

These settings take effect after you relaunch Motion

Default Project Settings: Set the default duration for a new Project (in frames or seconds).

The Background parameter in the Projects Properties settings has to be set to "Solid" in order to display the Background Color that you select here with the color well.

Select the behavior when opening a new Document (Project). Choose to open the Project Browser or a default Project that you define with the *Choose* button.

Still images & Layers: Set the default duration for any Object that doesn't contain a duration (graphics, generator, shape, etc). Set it to a custom length or the duration of the Project.

Only dragging Objects to the Timeline lets you define the start position of that Object. Any other import method needs a start information (Current Playhead position or first frame of your Project).

The Large Stills popup menu lets you choose to scale those files to fit the Canvas Size, or keep their original aspect ratio.

▶ **Time**

Time Display: Set the Time Display to show frames or seconds and start a Project from either 0 or 1.

Playback Control: The Time View popup menu lets you choose the behavior in the Timing Pane. If the Playhead reaches the right edge of the Timing pane, it just continues and you wont' see it anymore (*Don't update*) or the Timing Pane automatically scrolls one page to the right so you can follow the Playhead (*Jump by pages*). With the third option (*Scroll continuously*), the Playhead stays constant when it reaches the middle of the Timing Pane and now the Timing Pane scrolls underneath the static Playhead.

The other three settings let you choose the behavior when Audio sync is lost, limit the playback speed to your Project frame rate and turn off the audio loop while scrubbing (opt+drag the Playhead).

Keyframing: The first checkbox lets you lock the Keyframe in time (horizontally) to allow only value changes (vertically) for the Keyframes. The second checkbox allows a finer timing resolution in subframes for Keyframes.

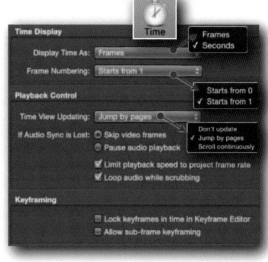

▶ **Cache**

Memory & Cache: Set the maximum amount of System Memory used by Motion in percentage. Higher number allows for smoother rendering of your Project but is a trade off when forcing the system to increase its swap files when running out of physical memory.

Autosave: Motion doesn't use the new system controlled autosave that was introduced with *Versioning* in OSX 10.7. The settings in this section configures the standard autosave behavior.

Optical Flow Retiming: Motion stores the retiming files on your computer when you retime footage. This section lets you choose the location of those files, either in the same location with the source media or at a custom defined location.

▶ **Canvas**

The Canvas pane has two tabs, Alignment and Zones.

Alignment: This section lets you set the *Grid Spacing* and *Grid Color* and the color for the two types of Guides, the Dynamic Guides that use any existing Objects or items in your Canvas and the Manual Guides (just called Guides) that you create manually in your Canvas. Two popup menus let you select the Snapping behavior and the Ruler Location. Please remember this is for the snapping mode in the Canvas not the other snapping mode that is used in the Timing Pane.

Zone: The two sliders set the Action Safe and Title Safe margins plus the color for the Zone guides. The Film Zone popup menu provides a selection of standard aspect ratios and another color well sets the color for the film guides.

► **3D**

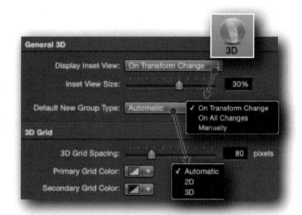

General 3D: The first popup menu sets the behavior for the Inset View which has to be enabled in the View Menu of the Canvas. You can choose to have it displayed when you edit any parameters (*On All Changes*), the Transform parameters only (*On Transform Changes*) or set it to be always visible (*Manually*). The slider sets the size of the Inset view in percentage.

The *Default New Group Type* settings let you choose if a new Group will be set to *2D* or *3D*. When set to *Automatic*, Motion decides the type based on the Project, if it is primarily in 3D or 2D.

3D Grid: Set the *3D Grid Spacing* with the slider and the *Primary* and *Secondary Grid Color* with the color well.

► **Presets**

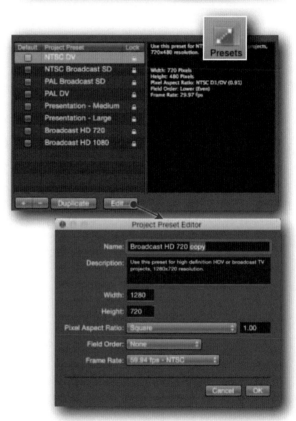

This list displays presets for various Project Settings. All those presets will be part of a popup menu in the upper right corner of the Project Browser that lets you select a specific setting when creating a new Project. The Default checkbox lets you select which preset will be pre-selected in that popup menu. All those settings can be changed later in the Project Properties (**cmd+J**).

The summary box on the right displays the Project properties for the selected preset.

All the factory presets are locked, but you can duplicate them first to create a custom preset if you want to edit them. With the plus and minus buttons, you can also add or remove presets from the list. The Edit button opens the selected preset in the *Project Preset Editor* window where you configure the preset.

► **Gestures**

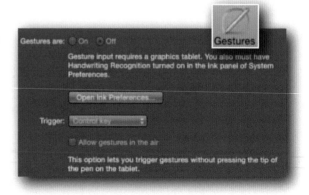

This window lets you configure a Wacom Intuos graphics tablet to use with Motion. The controls are inactive when you don't have the device connected to your machine.

Conclusion

This concludes my "Motion 5 - How it Works" manual.

You can find more of my "Graphically Enhanced Manuals" on my website at: www.DingDingMusic.com/Manuals

Subscribe to my mailing list for updates and future releases: subscribe@DingDingMusic.com

All the titles are available as pdf downloads from my website, as printed books on Amazon.com and as Multi-Touch eBooks on Apple's iBookstore.

(languages: English, Deutsch, Español, 简体中文)

If you find my visual approach of explaining topics and concepts helpful, please recommend my books to others or maybe write a review on Amazon or the iBookstore. This will help me to continue this series.

Special thanks to my beautiful wife Li for her love and understanding during those long hours of working on the books. And not to forget my son Winston. Waiting for him during soccer practice always gives me extra time to work on a few chapters.

More information about my day job as a composer and links to my social network sites: www.DingDingMusic.com

Listen to my music on www.SoundCloud.com/edgar_rothermich/

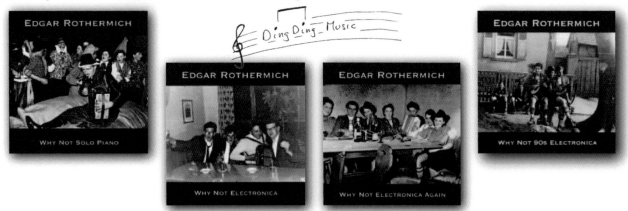

To contact me directly, email me at: GEM@DingDingMusic.com

Thanks for your interest and your support,

Edgar Rothermich

Printed in Great Britain
by Amazon.co.uk, Ltd.,
Marston Gate.